MOSAIC

NEW AND COLLECTED POEMS

by
Robin White Turtle Lysne

Copyright 2017
All rights reserved

Cover by: Robin Lysne
Interior Drawings by: Robin Lysne

ISBN # 978-0-9778645-9-1
Lbrary of Congres #: 2017949575

Mosaic New and Collected Poems
by Robin Lysne
Published with all rights reserved
by the author

Editors: Marcia Adams
Robin Lysne
Janet Trenchard
Blue Bone Books Cooperative

Published by:

Blue Bone Books
(A Cooperative Poetry Press)
P.O. Box 2250
Santa Cruz, CA 95063

www.BlueBoneBooks.com

Previously Published Poems

The following poems have been published in the sidebars of the non-fiction book *Heart Path, Learning to Love Yourself and Listening to Your Guides,* Blue Bone Books, Santa Cruz, CA 2007:
Birthday, Prow to Bow, Love Clouds, Sanctuary, Backyard Vision Quest, Healing Art, Night Mind, Red-Tail Lessons, Cocoon, The Gods Are Melting, Silver Thread, Immersion, Honey Strand, (also published on my website) Seed Change, The Muse Finds Me, Wolf Medicine, We like the Lilies, May Haiku, Cat Dream, Massaging This Turtle, Cruising, Looking Up Through Trees, Sunflowers Like Stars, Fog in the Morning, Pond Lilies, The Writer and The Mother Finally Talk.

The following poems were also published in the Emerald Street Anthology *Harvest from the Emerald Orchard*:
Prow to Bow, Rasberry, Bear Nights and Sterling Moons, Roots and Rice, Pacheco Pass, Honey Strands, 2007
Roots and Rice - Porcupine Literary Magazine, 1997
First Step - Dancing Up the Moon, published by Conari Press, 1995, used at the bench dedication for the survivors of Virginia Tech massecure 2010
Last Massage - Korone, Woman's Voices Vol. VIII 1994
Carrion Hunters-Korone, Woman's Voices Vol.IX, 1996
Luxurious Release (Now titled-Emersion)-Wet Poet's Society, James Miller, ed. Redwood Wedding - Tree Stories, Warren Jacobs, Karen Shragg, eds., also Dancing Up the Moon, Conari Press, Berkeley.
Blue Bones-Korone, Woman's Voices Vol.X 1998
Death of the Death Wish – North American Review, September - October Issue Volume 290-Number 5, 2005
Love Cars - Sand Canyon Review, 2012.
The Golden Bell - Awakening Consciousness Magazine, 2012
Jasmine Pearl-Heart Path Handbook, An Energy Medicine Guide, 2014
Friend to A Friend, Night Thorns, Love Cars-Pren-Z Literary Magazine, 2014.
Blank and Blue, El Camino Real - Porter Gulch Review, 2016
Canyon Flight, Inscriptions - Monterey Poetry Review, Fall, 2016
What the Sea Does for Us, WInter Night Walk, Well Within, Awe on East Cliff, A Range of Ranges Appointment with the Wild - Phren-Z Literary Magazine, 2016,
Cape of Ulysses, and Carrion Flower - Sand Canyon Review 2017

Table of Contents

Previously Published Poems	3
Table of Contents	4
Dedication	10
Roots and Rice - Drawing: Roots	**12**
First Step	13
Roof Child	14
Roots and Rice	15
Another Neverland	16
Premonition #1 and Premonition #2	18
Premonition #3	19
Post Office Revival	20
Happy Birthday Edith Joyful	22
Mosaic	25
For Nick	26
Passage	28
Guns and Oceans of Grief	29
Grief Group	30
The Decision	30
The Pool Man	32
Dennis Russell Davies Conducting	33
Conductors	34
At the Met -God Bless Noguchi	35
Love Cars	36
Blank and Blue	37
Traveling Sales Man	38
Beach Closed	40
Appointment with the Wild	41
Awe on East Cliff	42
A Range of Ranges	43
Well Within	44
Drawing: Coy with Reflections	45
Winter Night Walk	46
What the Sea Does for Us	47
Bear Nights and Sterling Moons	48
Rite of Passage	50
A Glympse of Heaven	51
Treasure	52
Mother's Plates	53

Tail Fins	54
Generations Fly Before Us	55
Sketches	56
Los Angeles de la Muerte	57
Why We Don't Speak Ill of the Dead	58
The End of the Story	60
El Camino Real	61
The First Supper	62
Fish School	64
Wedding Rite	65
Sinking My Hands	66
Coming Home	68
Blue Box of Memories	69
Blue Bones	70
Collapse	72
Ashes	74
Brave Ones	75
The Gods are Melting	76
The Turning	77
Closing the House	78
Poem for Jeanine Kalica	79
Insriptions	80
Reunion	81
Birthday	82
Work Week	84
Pacheco Pass	85
Encounter	86
Dream of the Last Tapestry	87
Iowa River 500 Year Flood Blues	88
Fences	89
Touching Center	90
A Perfect Flight	91
Finding Each Other	92
Raven Man	94
For Kathleen	97
Brave	98
The Animal Man	99
Bird Memories	99
Lost and Found	100
Sliver of Anger	101

Etheriate	102
Love Clouds	103
I Go My Own Way	104
After Candlemas	105
God Parents	106
Ode to Hatsy	107
Trick or Treat	108
Jodell	109
Cape of Ulysses	109
A Cold Promise	110
Baby Porcupine	111
No Bread	112
Bombs over Baghdad	113
Reverberations	114
Lanterns	116
Succulant Art Collection	117
Bartering at the Border	118
Nappying with Minka	119
Big Birds	119
Stone Circles	120
Last Massage	122
Shades Apart	124
Cat Time	125
Carrion Hunters: Drawing: Tex Pelvis Flying	126
Prow to Bow	127
Pond Lily	128
I-90 Pit Stop	130
Rasberry	130
Field Hands	131
Hummingbird	131
Babies and Buckeys	132
Mother of Pearl Moon	133
Carrion Hunters	134
Two Autumns	135
Casa Blancas	136
One Mornng I Found...	136
Last Tilling	137
How Callas Were Made	138
Callas	139
Wish	140

Calla	141
Morning Feed	142
Breakfast	144
El Flamboyán	145
Crack, Bang, Boom	146
Hot Springs Archeology	147
We live with the Geese I	147
We live with the Geese II	148
First Winter Frost	149
Winter Migration	150
Sun Down	150
Solstice	151
Dec. 25	151
Cannea and Calla	152
Looking Up Through Trees	153
Morning Ritual Walk	154
On the Altar of Trillum	155
May Haiku	156
Stellar Bird	158
Sunflowers Like Stars	159
Naná-Fresh Water Spring	160
Chili Pepper Love	161
Pacific Rim	162
Rain, Rain	163
The New Road	164
Risk	166
Desert Moon	169
Music	169
Sanctuary	170
Wake-Robin	172
Moon Mirrors	174
Fog in the Morning	175
The Emerald Self - Drawing: Rising Lilies	**176**
Stained Glass Sun	177
The Emeralds Self	178
Redwood Wedding	178
Owl Medicine	179
Carrion Flower	180
Star Baby	181
White Turtle Woman, The Earning of My Name	182

The Master and the Miser	184
Red Baby Blue	185
Past Life Lie-1753- Reclamed 2005	186
Sprout	188
Sundance	189
Extinction of the Phoenix	190
Honey Strands	191
What I Know About Mariluna	192
What Promises have you Made?	193
Hum of the Earth	194
Immersion	195
The Muse Finds Me	196
Sparrow	198
Neptunes's Church	199
Traveling Towards Dawn	200
Firelight	201
Turtle Massage	202
Masseur	204
Norma's Dream	205
For Those who are New to Grief	206
Ewa	207
Illusion of Blue	208
What We Don's Say	210
Night Thorns	211
Fukushima Mon Amour	212
Before the Phoenix	213
Death of a Death Wish	215
Silver Thread	216
Dessert Walk	217
Star Woman	218
Impression	219
Water WIndows	220
Drawing: Reflections	221
The Writer and the Mother Finally Talk	222
Be Careful What You Say to Yourself	226
Cat Dream	227
Backyard Vision Quest	228
Cocoon	230
Beloved	232
Night Mind	233

Healing Art	234
Ode to the Orishas	236
Red-tail Lasson	238
Sitting in the Meditaion Hall	239
Affinty Sign	240
Wolf Medicine	241
Jasmine Pearl	242
White Spectacle	243
Pin Point	244
Sunrise Art Flight	245
Water Cradle	246
Seed Change	247
The Sirens of Avila	248
Emersion	249
The Waters are Black Silk	250
I Step into her Shadow	251
New Years Day Resolution	252
The Sound of Petals	253
Cruising	254
This Emerald Man	255
The Promise of Attention	256
On Fire	258
My Hands Will Never Grow Tired	259
Arrival	260
The Golden Bell	262
Painting: Self-Portrait as Star Woman	263
About the Author	264
Acknowledgements	265

Dedication

**For the Sistas
in my many communities
and in my family
who inspired
many of these poems**

MOSAIC

NEW AND COLLECTED POEMS

by
Robin White Turtle Lysne

ROOTS AND RICE

First Step

Beginnings
  are sometimes foggy.
The path is not always clear.
    The end of one begets another.

To begin, put one foot
   in front of the other.
Your foot knows where to land,
   the one that moves forward first.
Forget about the best foot.

Just put it out there.
    Stop traffic if you have to.
Go home if that is where it leads you.
Go back to work
   if that is where your foot falls.

You don't have to
go anywhere.
   Just rest.
After you step,
   take another.
Forget about the whether,
  Step.
   Step again.

Roof Child

On the roof of our two story house
before the first summer storm
I am careful to sit below
the lightening rod.

                              Next to the chimney is safe,
                          the bricks will protect me, I say
                                  to my nine year-old self.

No one below can see me.

                        Yet, up here I see the tops of houses,
                              Oaks, and Walnuts
                             where the other Robins nest.

I see how the wind turn leaves over
makes their white palms
raise in praise,

                                          how the birds
                                  pull their wings back
                              darting in the wild winds.

At the first cracking open of sky,
I am electric with lightening bolts running
through the random air.

                                          rain splatters
                                          giant drops

then stops

                  thunder stirs me

                                      on the edge
                                        up high,
                                  I close my eyes,

imagine that I am
taken by the wind
soaring wild.

Roots and Rice

Father, how we have smoothed that black stone passed between us,
    the years of polishing water mixed with sand.

Is this the last dance we take around our ancestral tree?
    As we move, I perceive how deep the root of you is in me.

Branches sprout from my head, blossoming now
    from your not-so gentle pruning.

Yet your white bird dreams have taken flight through your daughters
    while grandchildren live their wildest crow careening.

This ancient conflict we've maintained: Science as the way for you,
    the dark silence of the pond for me,

You still want to pound me with your measuring stone
    yet the flour of this self is made for poems.

Besides, we have come to the end of pricing
    and dividing these grains of rice.

There is nothing more to say,
    just one last long walk through this winter garden.

Two old fools arm in arm, circling around a black bowl of
    white rice,

Who laugh and spin again
    this ancient sign of wholeness.

Another Neverland

In here, I am Wendy and they are
the lost boys, though I have my badge,
they have county uniforms.

They sit around me in
'Substance Abuse Recovery"
with my stories, and theirs.
They love class
though they complain.

They smile, their bright faces turn up.
If they could lay on their bellies
chins in their hands, feet in the air crossing
and uncrossing, they would.

Instead, they squirm in steel chairs,
and around metal tables.
They have come to hear
uncomfortable tales

of absent fathers,
drunk mothers,
how their girlfriends
haven't written in weeks.

Like anxious children,
they learn bits about each other,
the mystery of
their adventures that landed them in here.

One speaks of his first taste of laced brownies
at age 5, how bikers and hippies
met at parties at Mom's.

One is shattered by the death
of his Dad at age 8, another lost his job,

his home, his wife, then kids
all in one year.

Towards the end of class every night,
I take them on the journey of their lives.
Inside themselves they enter their own gardens.
We meet their wild animals,

find their own Wendys and Peters,
as Tinkerbell hovers over head, then they
confront Captain Crook.

They nestle inside themselves around campfires,
as they pass the talking stick to speak private
truths they've known but never
dared utter out loud.

And when they are done, I stamp
their passes and sheets.

They leave this island
we created together
for a game of cards, a shower,
the weight room or treats.

As I leave one whispers
his new discovery
that hidden under dark roots
he just unlocked an old trunk
and out popped
his own lost boy.

Premonition #1

I haven't met you yet,
       though I hear you calling
as clear as a hawk screech
       cutting through winter air
I hear you running towards me
       on a horse down a shallow creek
along the wall of red canyons

Premonition #2

Sun sketches its way between limbs
a bright orb held aloft in oak shadows.

It becomes my crystal ball
a long road to somewhere

two worlds merge, one deep in snow
one here where this sun lowers

wind whirling across plateaus
then California greening in winter

two worlds overlapping through
one sun telescope blurring, then clear.

Premonition #3

The picture you sent,
a ketch sailing off into
the early orange night
black clouds darkening all
but your single boat,

remind me that your 87 years,
are strong yet waning.
Your soul longs for the sunset,
your Viking ship farewell.

In my heart I hand you a rose,
I wish you the best, Dad,

Odd, how Mom did the same;
announced her death
with a sunset painting,
hers by the lake with dark trees
making a kaleidoscope
to the end of the water.

My sisters know too,
and we are giving out
our whereabouts
just in case of emergency.

Post Office Revival

Plexi-glass one inch thick between you and
postal worker
I take a number, 27,
there are seven people missing
from the red number
lighted above the window.

Inside this red and grey cement building,
ringing the sameness of each one of us
no matter who we are, no matter if we are
the lost numbers seem to fit.

Grasp the woman in dreadlocks and tennis shoes
she wants them to tape her package,
she wants them to tell her she is going somewhere,
she wants them to take her through
the window and mail her anywhere else.

A black grandfather next to me,
and his Chinese daughter in law,
with her small child,
talk in uneasy conversation.

The adults are not close,
but the child bridges them,
unites Africa, and China
in an uneasy conversation.

However you look at it
this place receives people
and lets them go except for

Two Mexican men who come in trying for a visa
no one is there at five o'clock on Friday to help them.
They bounce off the window and out to the street.

A crazy man in white dreads,
fear covering his face,
runs in, looks around, looks in shock
and shocks a few himself. His ghost
leaves suddenly mumbling
then he shouts something on the street
to bring himself back in, then stumbles away.

This is not a post office I want to return to,
save for one man behind the plexi-glass.
He is bright, he is wanting to greet the God in you
he booms over the loud speaker:
"Number a ah 27!"

"How are you today." he snapping his head to the side
really wanting an answer.
"Just fine" I say.
"That's Good, REAL GOOD!"
He gives everyone a chance to pray
while he stamps my letter with care,
while he tells me the cost and smiles.

He is holding his own U.S. government
revival meeting with each soul
that he serves
inside the drab of this Post Office building.

"Thank you," I say.
"Thank YOU!" he replies.
"Have a great weekend," I wish for him.
As our eyes lock.

Over the loud speaker his voice booms,
"NUMBER uhum twenty-nine!"
He could be saying:
"Come blessed souls,
I am here to love you,
number or no number."

Happy 82nd Birthday Edith Joyful

We bonded over her bucket when I was twelve. I remember she would sweep this room, then dust that one following her own whim. I followed her from place to place and we would talk.

Today, this day, I call her in the same nursing home where Grandma died thirty years before. She takes a long time to get to the phone. Her step shuffles behind her walker she fumbles the receiver.

"Robby, dat you? Well, if it ain't my sweet angel. All the way to California! My, my, my."

Her speech is slow then more rapid, a prisoner of her body and this place.

"Sorry to call after your birthday Edith, but it is crazy out here, Dad sent me pictures." I say apologetically.

Undaunted by the lateness of my call to her actual birthday she carries on. "Robby, don't you never mind. Do you know, dat old boy tricked me. Social service gonna fix up my house."

The old boy is my Dad, who pulled his medical strings to get her here. She's been told a thousand times her house has been condemned. She's been here for three years now.

"Just fine for me an Tanrio." The septic tank was under the rotting bathroom floor.

There was no running water. She threw the sewage out the window. Tanrio is her niece's boy who she had from a few months old until he got too big, until he wouldn't mind her any more. She raised all the others there too, his mother, and her mother, her son and his other cousins, all in that tiny house one at a time, on a house keeper's salary.

In the photos Dad sends me of this year's birthday party one shows her smiling with her cake that he brought her. "Happy Birthday Edith Joyful" was elegantly spelled out in turquoise and pink. Sugar roses and yellow daffodils arch across thick white frosting. In this picture she's smiling, her hair brushed back not straightened.

"Those white girls can't straighten my hair, needs a black girl to do this old nigger's doo." she chuckles.

In the next picture, Edith sits in a chair, my Dad sitting next to her in his chair holding the cake. Still in his jacket, always ready to leave, his age shows under his captain's cap. Her mouth is a

straight tight line. In another photo Edith holds the cake between two lady friends. The ladies hold stuffed animals. Both are in wheel chairs, one is white and has rouge and pink lipstick. The other woman is mulatto and smiles slightly.
Edith wears purple sneakers and rolled white socks, her feet dangle from the chair. Her bulbous breasts hang at her waist under her flowered dress. Her t-shirt over her dress says: *Mother* with garands of flowers around the word. Her golden brown skin is thin and soft as always. Her eyes are sad and dim. Bags hang down under her eyes.
"That Alzheimer's look," my Dad often remarks. He always taught diagnosing from pictures. He sends me pictures every year from her birthday photo. Every year she has a more hollow look. Every year she slips a little further away.
This birthday, she has a necklace of russet beads that match her dress. I look at the photos as I listen. Her knurled hands show the wear of scrubbing my mother's floors, turning her rag over and over.
When she cleaned years before this photo, she'd tell me about her boyfriend, or the kids she was raising. I would tell her about school, and friends, an occasional boyfriend. When her knees hurt too much to stand up, she'd say, "Robby hands me dat cleaner woulds ya? Oh that's my sweet angel."
She looked me in the eye then, as she still does, but not my Mom. To Mom, she'd bow her head and look down at her shoes. With Grandma it was worse. She'd almost crawl around the house under my Grandma's southern drawl. "Yes, Miss Lysne," she'd say then obey. Both my Grandma and Mom hated the cultural conditioning that created her behavior, understood it too. My Grandma just would look at me with her wide gray eyes and shrug.
"At least they've got black nurses aides." Dad reports in a recent phone call. "There are other elderly blacks there her age too. It's clean, they take care of the people. She'll be okay." He is six years her elder and still on his own at 88.
"Nobody's like Edith." I say to him on occasion.
She worked for thirty some years for my parents until three

years after Mom's death, until she couldn't stand the missing of her, and her knees finally gave out at 78.
She worked for other doctors' families too. Mrs. Daniels had Edith for forty-five years. Mark moved his mother to Tennessee and Dad connects them on his cell phone.
He is her only visitor now, not the ladies from her church, not Tanrio, not even Edith's son, though he lives now with someone else and can't drive himself to the Eastside. He can't drive, he is disabled from too many strokes.
"I'm way over here, my people are on the Westside, what am I doing over here?" She says. Then recants how she is going home, how social service is fixing up her house.
"That ol' dog!" She says for the tenth time.
Dad has become the Man, her white slave holder, her nemesis.
"Took all my money, and only gives me twenty dollars." She protests. She doesn't remember that she might get it stolen from other senile residents, or that her own kids and grand children have robbed her blind on rare visits.
"Oh Edith, he is just keeping it safe for you." I say, knowing he's trying to protect her.
"Mrs. Daniels, she sent me a lot more than dat."
"He'll give you more if you want it." I say.
"He tricked me, said we was going for a ride. We came here instead. I never wants to come here." She has no other place to go.
Then she softens.
"Robby? You's my sweet gal. I loves you like you was my own."
Then she tells me one more time about her money, her house and Tanrio coming back.
"I just wants to go home." She finally says, "I just wants to go home, Robby."
"I know, you will, just close your eyes and you'll be there, Edith."
"Robby, don't tell that ol' dog, but honey, I'm striving everyday to make heaven my home. I loves you, Robby."
"I love you too, Edith." I loves you like you was my own.

Mosaic

We entered into
a new stadium
where the games begin.

The women referees on the side lines
 were speaking poorly
about men.

I looked past them
to the wall
near the goal.

We were the mosaic
facing each other.

Tiles of gold,
blue and silver,
violet, red, yellow glisten.

The scene behind us,
a pond with two cranes
taking flight,

'That is what I want,' I said.
The other women
did not hear me,

but you did. So we joined hands
and floated into it
becoming the art in my dream.

For Nick

Brave new comedian
courage suits you
to light your own way.

You collaborate on comedy
with other young fools like you.
Everyone has a second job.

You wait tables
she runs bar codes over lasers at Safeway
He picks up packages for U.P.S.

At night you settle together on the
imaginary stage like a flock of crows
always at the White Raven tavern.

You use the salt shaker for him
the pepper for her
sugar becomes her part
as together you push and pull the taffy

Of comedy off
each other's palms
and spoon with delight
the meringue of collaboration.

Late into the night
you can't stop laughing at each other's jokes
no one can write them down
on little cocktail napkins fast enough.

The waitress brings another round
and more napkins
to sop up the spray
tears of beer run down your cheeks
your sides ache from laughing too much.

You know the joy of peer confluence
when everything clicks and making is the sweet rhythm
of your comedy skit born around midnight,

And you are getting $134 a week
just enough to pay Minnesota heating bills in Spring.
Who cares? You are 22 saving for retirement
is someone else's folly.

Brave New Workshop writer,
my poem of praise – what better joy
could I ask for you?

Passage

Mathew sits in the garage on his skateboard
and sews canvas for his newest creation.
He stiches together
army surplus riveted canvas
and rose covered patches of upholstery cloth.

Rolling back and forth on his low stool
he is not quite a man on his own
weaving rosy mannish khaki eyelets
he hooks more cloth in soft folds
through those holes.

He tugs and stitches the corners
clamps them with my canvas clamps
so his gender intention won't slip.
He grimaces, stops breathing,
rearranges himself on his rolling platform.

He stiches in his questions:
How does love fit with work?
When am I going to take off,
finance my way out of here?

How does Buddha blend with
Cathedrals and that circle of stones?
Where is mine to draw
my chalk circle

what rituals do I want
to make for myself?
Who is my tribe?

Guns and Oceans of Grief

A hand pushes you under. It flows, surges, gushes until you cannot stand it. The pain is exquisite beyond anything you could imagine. Your pain is so sharp, you can't take it because no one wants to feel it and here you are plunged in without any choice. Plunge into it, pushes you under. Guns kill 19 children a day.

There is no choice but to lay there, bleeding, drowning. You feel as though the life will run out of you, you weep, you weep, and suddenly the rain stops and the flood water stop. You are released for a moment. You rise long enough to see the sky breaking above you.
Guns kill 19 children a day.

But the loss is still there. That ache so deep you think that all will be drained down the hole of it. So gargantuan you cannot breathe it in and release it, you just grieve. And grieve. There is no bottom. Then the shallower tears come. They are penetrating the crust of resistance you have, piercing your chest. Making your life deeper, wider, running among the stores of pain. Oceans of it. Guns kill 19 children a day.

You weep so much you realize that there is nothing but this grief. You dig so deep you reach the center of the Earth where everyone's roots grow from the ocean hidden inside her. This is where they bury everything they do not wish to feel, then they are touched by your tears and don't want you or anyone to be reminded, so they say, never mind, never mind, it can't be that bad. Guns kill 19 children a day.

Feeling everything, everything, then this grief of loss of a child or a spouse or of your dog would not be so big, would not come with such intensity, nor dominate everything, sweep away your house, flood the canyon. Tear the rocks clean from where they have rested precariously for generations. Guns kill 19 children a day.

The only way to survive the pain is to make it your friend. Like an obnoxious person, you make them your friend, then you understand why they can't cope normally. And we relax, we relax in the sea, float upon it, it meets every shore anyway. But you say it is not your shore, you could not hold your breath long enough to reach the bottom anyway.

The sea sings with you, this water is made for sailing if you can reach the surface. Guns kill 13 children a day.

And you want to cause more flooding?
Guns kill 19 children a day.

Grief Group

The children float together
after their Tsunami has struck.
They float and stare at the sun gazing up
looking towards heaven
some rollover like fish and search the bottom
for answers they drift with the tides
all day they float asking why.

They swim to this boat
still no answers, then
one child ties a message to her Grandparents on a balloon,
another sends a whole painting, folds it up, ties it on tight
and releases the balloon to a father somewhere
up and up.

Every night we close the circle in the same way,
wait for parents to come join hands
someone starts a love squeeze
until it's passes all around the circle
making our raft.

The Decision

In my dream you and I
were unwinding streams
releasing the invisible child
brought through you Carpenter
me Artist.

I would have been bound to you,
and instead had to let you go.

Still, the birth of a child, what a miracle

despite your cutting ways,
your disregarding tongue.
I did not want your harshness
for them or me any more.

In my dream I watch the unwinding
of that invisible cord, the strand
of generations weaving together

a single decision to let go the dream

and I wake rocking in the reality of
it will never be.

The Pool Man

He scoops the long pole
bent by water
in a slow curling motion.
A net on the end catches
leaves by surprise
sweeps them into another world.

He has done this many times
twisting his wrist
in an effortless winding,
a master hypnotized by the
water's resistance.

When he is done,
the pool is bright again,
a blue kidney to
match a dazzling sky.

Dennis Russell Davies Conducting
Dvorak Symphony No. 8 in G Minor, Op.88

He rattles his baton
and gathers together the warp
and weft of the symphony. Now he
smooths the withers of his horse,
punches bread dough and divides it,
stirs storm clouds and
releases the thunder and the rain.

In the second movement, he rocks
an infant to sleep, now sews
Belgium lace,
casts a handful of seeds,
thrashes wheat then
gathers the grain to taste of it.

Now he strokes his beloved's face
embraces an old friend, and
scolds his son.

Finally from between the
webbing of his fingers
he draws out a single thread.
On a spindle he thins it and
weaves the clouds together. Then
he presents the steaming hot loaf
on a table set with a vase of
Calla Lilies.

All this without a score
drawn from the bones
of the maestro.

Conductors

Barenboin's rooster hand flares
above his head.
Now he is a stork
first straight and alert,
then he bows,
      a dignified long arch
           into a deep translucent pool.

Davies arms are as fluid as this phrase;
A bird wing lifts in slow motion,
now rises higher in one large
flap and swoop - first a hawk,
now a fluttering sparrow, then
a tiny hummingbird
      rapidly beating it's invisible wings.

The maestro holds on to nothing
in the moment but this;
the heat of summer, and the bitterness
of winter, violent spring rains,
the orange and reds of autumn leaves,
and in between each phrase, lacing flight
      over vast fields of burgeoning
           silence.

At the Met - God Bless Noguchi

On the second floor, beyond
the room of Japanese furniture
beyond the Hiroshige paintings,
a sculpted stone of water glistens,
a seven-sided crystal
with a perfect circle
cut into it's core.
Black basalt, wet
but not a splash
every side
designed
to shimmer,
to quiver fluidly,
authentically, and
if you listen carefully,
you can hear a faint trickle
dripping off its black bottom
to a gray bed of round river rocks.
Those drops you barely hear circulate
- though clearly through midnight
as through a new moon -
and somehow
rise
without a ripple
to join
the flat perfect puddle on top,
- a deep black circle -
of which I cannot stretch to see the center.
Though the platform around the stone
prevents it,
any one drawn to the core,
would want to step up and look down,
to the source of the deepest waters.

Love Cars

You make me better. How the thought before
the poem, how it changes after

Ambling skunks and an elderly heiress who
buys up land in her view, how painting or poetry make my day,

then the quaking hour, when
tell-tale signs sing out of those love cars

on Lowell's hill, you make me quake
when I think about it, the two of us in one

a shiver that went through you earlier that day
as we walked past the young black model

posing on the beach with her cadre. We welked sideways
as crabs in a borrowed residence, ogling her.

I saw your shiver, and I felt my opposition, white
edging sixty, wrinkles, and you squeeze my hand

as we talked about a place to pee, another beach, dinner, oysters or
those black muscles maybe. Still you make me shiver

when I think you, of this tenuous moment,
how either one of us could turn away any time,

though after dinner, we were the ones in the love cars off
Highway 1 dangling near a cliff edge scooping love bites

from seaweed, shivering in each other's sex. That is when you
mentioned love cars, how we were in one, in Lowell's poem at the
same time.

You enliven me with those skunks, your muscles
in their brown skin, rippling as you touch me, hand to my breast.

Blank and Blue

Blue was behind you, blue covered the blank sky
you were a cut out, not yet a memory,
then the memory faded, it came
open, the blue shade, when you stepped on the cord
and behind was air where you
were cut out. It wasn't sky it wasn't there after all.
Curtains in waves met me, met you.

Blank was the fact
that you had slept somewhere else the night before,
though you didn't sleep together, you say.
How you are just that, confused. A blank slate
there in your chest from your wife who left.
Marriage became a habit, you say, of 30 years.

White blank wall is in my chest as you talk.
We are not blank slates, none of us,
even when we come into this world
and we don't just start over every week,
we continue, even if the cut-out has begun,
though the fields
are more golden out that window
and we are here inside a blue room tonight.

Through the hedges of wanting certainty
those boundaries we've made aren't even real, 'cause
being in this moment does not mean the next.
Still we empty our cups all week just to fill them again
in each other, because we can't keep our hands off the other.

Even so, after the blankness faded,
and we were still falling back
into bed and those white curtains lifted, even after you
pulled the cord down on the blank shade,
as the breeze blew over us,
we were more tender with each other than ever.

Traveling Salesman

A desk, a table lamp,
a chair and suitcase rack.

Two light bulbs
are burned out
though there
is a good shower head,
a firm mattress,

the switch by the
door doesn't work
with any appliance.
The T.V. has 33 channels.

The pictures are too small for the walls
the mirrors offset, this room says,
'rest tonight, but tomorrow,
good-bye, have a nice trip.'

I imagine I am a traveling salesman
driving from one dull room to the other
the sheets are clean, and where
would I find a place I could have just one,

a drink, a girl,
but tomorrow I have ten offices to visit
and then one more night on the road
before I return to

screaming kids and a wife,
the grass in the yard over grown
the roof needs fixing.

And what has life come to,
traveling from place to place,
selling one more widget
to make my quota?

So, here I am, not a man, nor a salesman,
just a woman on the road imagining
who might have slept here last night,
a picture of the grand canyon
dangling above this same bed.

Beach Closed
Capitola Beach, Santa Cruz County, 3/11/2017

I watch another family straddle the same sign
to explore what winter has washed in.
Logs tossed like matchsticks
are made into t-pees, and children duck in
and out to play hide and seek.

There must be all races of people out there
their children exploring what they find,
turning over shells, picking up sticks,
looking for treasures.

It is a human happiness to beach comb.

A flock of pigeons peck the sand
and strut and chase after females
like those teenagers over by the rocks
chasing each other.

People break rules in Santa Cruz, it's our duty,
we do it together, as the sun is going down slowly,
even as some are leaving the beach one by one
except those surfers who jog their way through
logs and people to reach the waves,

and for some unknown compulsion, I sit here
amused and happy with them,
listening to Spanish and Farci, Hebrew, and Serbian,
African, Jive, and all of us together,

on this same plot of Earth and Sea and Sky
as one family who break the rules imposed on us.
And I am writing it all down furiously.

I *must* be their scribe.

Appointment with Wild

Drawn to the beach
as if by appointment
scanning the waves
just beyond the breakers

Something huge is out there
dolphins or whales or sharks
stirring up water
rolling over
first a fin then a tail
ribbony back diving.

Its too close to shore
yet too far away to see well
at least three spouts every
minute or two
clearly whales

The wild is so close
such a rubbery ballet
flukes and fins and a
nose out of the water
blow and twirl then dive.
Is this play full tilt or a shark attach?
Another fluke now a long back
with a ridge line spine diving

dozens of people stop and watch
one woman, shouts,
They're just too close!
and as if she commands it
one pod joins another
then suddenly, all of them turn out to sea.

A fin, a splash
a swirl, fading
I never tire of this
wild sea explosion.

Awe on East Cliff

Full sheen of moon
a silver bowl on
glittering wedge spilling out over
the Monterey Bay.
We walk for the exercise but are
stopped in our quick pace
to marvel at this light.
We lean on the rail off East Cliff Drive.
Waves roll and sparkle then become
a black curl to white foam lines
then dissolve
as our conversation
into sand.

A Range of Ranges

As Spring abates
the wild Yuba River gushes
so fast you might be swept away
if you get too close.

Hills shimmer green and lush
with wildflowers fed from
lakes and icepack rush.

On my way to the coast
the Central Valley has already
gone golden in mid-May.
Dry summer heat has taken hold.

Further on, along the coast range
gullies are green
where runoff has kept them in
their winter favor as
sunward sides turn tawny.

Back to the Santa Cruz Mountains
fog keeps redwoods and oaks
forever green and thick
on steep terrain.

Cool ocean air gusts
over Highway 17 as our summer pattern
begins to breathe mist
over everything.

Well Within
Santa Cruz, CA

Outside the spa   double Datura spiral open
their claw-petals turn up slightly.

As buds lengthen gradations appear from white to coral,
and blossoms rotate as a new-born star.

Inside I am led to my room where tea and two cups,
a towel, and a spa, with a gentle bubbling surface, invites.

Flute music sets the tone as I ease into the hot tub,
I soak for a while, then

with my arms over the transom of wood and paper screens
I delight in a Japanese garden outside.

A stand of black bamboo clacks in the breeze,
fish swim in a pond below.

I watch their movements,
relax my body.

A white coy swims under red maple leaves
and around a stand of grasses.

It noses the surface for food, its maw opening and closing
then swims around a golden one, a spotted one, a brown one.

I could watch them for hours as I move my legs
the same way as their fins then slide back into the spa to
float.

My hour is up. I shower and dress again. Feeling reborn
I slowly float out under the perfumed canopy of Datura

out the bamboo gate
stars glittering all the way through.

Coy with Reflections and Clouds

Winter Night Walk

Winter waves rise
from a steel plate surface
a dragon back uncurling
deep look into nothing

then it becomes too lazy
to fully rise up
utters collapse
into sheen
recedes and grows
again into another
attempt to rise

the dragon dies
Consumes my grief
itself and the
wicked way it rises
without warning.

What the Sea Does for Us

On the Monterey Bay
this long curve of
white sand and rolls of kelp lie
like sleeping mermaids,
head and one shoulder
a hip, a long fin
buried in sand.
Every part of it
could wash away
into the surf again.

Her exposed fin
grows another mermaid
who dives back into waves
through the briny sea
to rejoin her kind
through kelp forests
where seals and sea otters
swim and dive.

I roll to my side,
stretch hair up, mimic
her shape, long legs
out to touch the surf
they become fins,
as the stress from the week
washes away.
I let the sea
take it all,
how something in me
follows her
into emerald caverns.

Standing up to feel the powder sand
between bare toes,
all that was heavy is gone now
all that was
has washed away.

Bear Nights and Sterling Moons

Before I met you
my fields were wide and flat,
I wandered around for days screaming
   and singing my pain to the corn fields.

You changed my life forever, and said
"It is my left side where I hold my grief too."
I said "I see a bear and a buffalo, white as snow."

You said nothing
opened your clenched fist
 to two fetishes—a bear and a buffalo—
carved of white stone.

You fill me
with your darkness
from behind the stars

We play in forests
thick with redwoods
these mountains thick
with caves to hide in
and waterfalls
in which to bathe.

You bring me
   shade
and more rain.

We have seen
green Iguanas in Puerto Rico
blue waters of Salvador Bahia
   and the falls of Iguaçu.

We have traveled through
the loss of our daughter,
joys of our two sons
and near death of one.

Oh you fill me with
the darkness of underwater caves,
swimming through beds of kelp
ten thousand leagues of learning.

You remind me
   water teaches evaporation,
darkness is a silent relief,
the noon sun hides your shadow.

I remind you each of us chooses
the buffalo plains, or bear caves
one more day   each breath.

I feel all that has passed
you let it go
we climb together and   alone

with our two hands folded together
we can survive loss,   keep dancing,
and love just a little bit more.

Beyond our buffalo dreams
we fly wild
   in bear nights and sterling moons
we rest

filled with turquoise oceans
we dive
through ochre plains
we run.

Oh those peaks beyond peaks and always
   another mountain pass   we climb

and at the end of each day
we come to each other,
rest in the other's arms
      sublime.

Rite of Passage

Waves lapping in the channel,
bathing the young male whale,
bathing the kayaks that swim around him,
it is not unusual for whales
to be seen on these shores,
but for one to come into the harbor,

at the moment a father and son
are reassessing their life together,
at the moment when the father says,
*I release my burden of carrying your part
of this relationship. I release it to you
because today I see that you are a man.*

At that very moment the whale surfaces,
displays its broad tail, dives in slow motion
back under the brine, right where the two
were walking on the jetty,
and here they are now man and man,
walking together as the young whale sounds.

A Glimpse of Heaven

It is a tight "S' curve on a dirt road.
A pickup truck is turning towards me,
gun rack in the back. The only passenger
a young woman. She keeps her eyes on our bumpers
so the two cars don't collide.

Jésus, the driver, is obscured by her radiance.
He navigates the corner, her black hair caught
up in her eyes, mixed with rays from the sun.

Brushing her hair back with her free hand
her face reveals
all the compassion of Mary
holding her crucified son.

She sits next to him as mother,
lover, abundant embrace. He
young, lively and mean
doesn't know what he has in her yet.

He is a wild one for sure
and she can't save him,
though she'll try.

After we have rounded the corner
in my rear-view mirror I see
she moves closer to him on the bench seat
as he cradles her in one arm,
drives with the other

as I focus again on what is in front of me
driving north through their dust
they drive south through mine
in totally opposite directions.

Treasure

Looking at your son's collage of Autumn leaves, you read his little poem just below. I watch you hold it's lens through years 'til now.

Sitting down through all the layers of life with him you wonder, When did he decide to live with me? Was it that summer he made this, when he turned nine?

You say to me, I remember he met his first new friend when he came to visit that summer, announcing the move with a postcard he asked me to mail to his mother.

Was that boy the same friend who rode the bus with him, or the one he ran with from rehab six years later? Remember the turn around he made, how he served us on Mother's Day in his last chance rehab, Sí Se Puede?

Your lens refocuses to today, the most recent layer. You wonder out loud how he discovered Yoga, and the new girl he's met.

I say, 'Remember this last Christmas when we were all together with his mother, the 'do' rag dance he did, laughing at his old gang style? Remember how he waxed on and on about his college classes, literature he's read, his discovery of meditation?'

Holding the collage before you, you see him at all his different stages. You see that bright young face, his copper skin with deep black eyes, a tiny version of yourself, holding his treasure up for you to admire.

Mother's Plates

The first one slipped from my hand
onto the storage room floor

Suddenly I felt my heart break open, yes!
A vow I had made rose to my lips

I will not live my life like hers!
Look at the pattern once more

Blue Willow with that rounded bridge
of perfect lovers meeting in the ideal Pagoda.

The trees are heart shaped   the shrubs like
diamonds. The path perfectly laid of interlocking stones.

Then I remembered
you chose in the womb not to be like her.

Mother said don't feel anger or sadness
don't feel illusion shattering

see those perfect birds kiss in midair
how the man takes the woman as his queen.

I say smash her old china patterns
break something precious,

those plates you never used anyway,
leap over the bridge to your freedom.

Make your own way along the swift river,
there is a boat drifting away

that one is your boat,
swim to it   set sail!

Tail Fins

442, 1927 Pontiac, 1949 Dodge,
attached to a soda shop garage,
classic bubble fenders, polish and tailfins.

Hand-dipped ice cream in the front of the shop,
by an older gentleman with a checkerboard collar, and cap
scooping his fantasies; tropical rainforest,
superhero, and maple-nut supreme.

His wife adds up the total,
scoops up her homemade bar-be-que beef, and hot dogs,
lays down green relish, yellow mustard
and the red line of ketchup.

Her husband looks at the crowd lining up,
"Holy Cow, did a bus pull up?"
He has a smirk on his face.

One older customer quips,
"We thought we'd come in for ice cream
so you wouldn't think we were dead."
Her mouth line is flat.

The sting of silence mixes with bittersweet chuckles.
My young friend bits into the relish covered dog.
Tastes the tang of mustard.

This is southern Minnesota, a spot frozen in time,
the ice cream shop, the whitewashed garage of old cars,
still the most happening place in 30 miles,
just off I-90 outside of Blue Earth.

Generations Fly Before Us

You have to see in three dimensions,
when we slice through meringue
dive through the silent
white cathedrals.
Our wings, like spatulas,
shave through the puffs
of potential thunderheads.
Flaps lift and tilt our trajectory
just enough to aim down the canal of clouds,
glide along the broad thigh
of Lake Michigan
into Chicago, our destination.

Above the air strip, generations
of tiny lights hold hundreds of people,
suspend like fireflies
over broad strips of concrete.
Although runway lights are white not yellow,
we home in just as drawn to our destiny
like the male mate
of the female lighted fly.

As though let out of a jar,
134 passengers scatter into the suburbs.
Each trails behind stories,
from Viking wanderlust, to slavery,
gospel choirs to silent vigils,
drunkards and angry mothers,
absorbed into city blocks,
coiled and uncoiled
like chromosomes.

Sketches

Nothing will stop cancer
from killing my Mother

Except today the way
she talks to the birds
while adding a hint of red-orange
to the cheek of the Chinese baby
whose portrait she draws.

What will heal her soul
are those moments
as she lays on her pillow
and goes into the garden
of her heart to visit herself there,

the way I taught her to go in
to prune the vines,
to meet anyone she needs to
and complete what is required.

I can hold her hand and help her
separate flower from thorn,
scribe memories for her grandchildren,
sketch our versions of chickadees together.

I have traveled across country
to see them through this and
tonight my parents are out with friends

So I dine alone with Mom's cups and saucers
sit in her chair, slip on her sweater,
wonder how many days exactly
remain to savor.

Los Angeles de la Muerte

My sisters, Los Angeles,
bathe my Mother's arms and legs

wipe the dried tears from her eyes
dress her in her favorite satin gown.

My father hovers near the door, then checks her
pulse her breathing, pats her hand, her cheek.

They are getting her ready for the journey,
not far away nor a winding path.

Yet she inhales dust from the road
which gathers in her throat with every breath.

On the other side her mother, our Abuela,
sings to her with a host of others like her.

Their wings brush the arches of my sister's wings,
my father's. It is only a matter of time.

Why We Don't Speak Ill of the Dead

Mother, it all started with a phone call
from your sister
After the usual catching up
she spoke of the cruelty she felt from you.

I acknowledged her, felt the same myself,
said that I knew you knew too,
in your heart of hearts.

I tell your sister, let it go,
Mother has been dead for years,
she cannot hurt you anymore.
We say our goodbyes.

Now I feel you, Mother, hook into my back
You keep coming back to attack.
Though your job as my Mother ended long ago.

Your spirit is still around and tries
to hook your anger into the 'eye' in me
that says 'connection.'

It's an ancient hook and eye arrangement
having nothing to do with love.
I lift your hook away
unscrew the eye in my back,
recognize the attachment is over.

You try to hook in someplace else
I decline having been careful to chisel
all the other attachments away.

Pulling the cord down attached to your hook
I set my boundaries once again
this time nose to nose,

Stop! No more! It's over Mom. Be gone!

I call in my guardians to take you way.
Teach her not to invade me again please.

You are kicking and screaming into the light,
not the gentle mother you wanted to be in a body.
I am relieved to see you flail and kick into the sky.
At least you can get angry honestly now.

The tail and plume of a giant white bird
settles on my back protecting the holes where you got in.
It is stitched from the inside
covered over with impenetrable layers of feathers.

Inside this heart of this giant bird,
my mother self opens her arms to this beloved child.
The wolf and jaguar sit calmly on guard.

The End of the Story

There comes a time
 when it doesn't matter
        what happened or who abandon whom.

Who cares who wrote
        their name across your heart
emblazoned with the letters of their triumph.

The truth is;
you felt what you felt and that is how we are;
        wounded yet waiting to heal.

So, go ahead stand in the pain for one long
        ceremonious and uncertain moment. Then look
at your true face,

still loving you despite everything.

El Camino Real

He comes home, polishes his huge boots on newspapers
blackens them with stripes and his street name, E-X
"Ex."

It sounds like Ax which he likes. Hacking his way
into adulthood. He comes here to rest from his street life,
his wild vida-loca drug use life.

His father and I watch him show up from time to time.
We do not talk about recovery anymore,
or what he sees in his future. Right now
there is no future.

He has made it clear that he wants to rock on the edge of now,
like the blue moon that weeps from his arm.
He is running, screaming into the void of manhood
with a tattooed belly "Lopez" independence.

We keep a bed for him.
His older brother reports to us of sightings.
But no one lectures him, or asks him to
mow the lawn.

I cannot help but stroke his shaven head.
He towers over me as I hug him goodbye one more time
and say, take care, keep in touch, I love you.

He grabs his jacket.
I remind him about the papers and shoe polish.
He stuffs the black bottle into his pocket,
throws the papers into the fireplace. He is out the door
mounting his El Camino.

The First Supper

You and I are in our hacienda,
seats opposite ends of the long planks.
We toast each other and our friends.
Nothing exists for me but your eyes
the center of the fireball, of the earth,
the navel in the ocean,
clouds gathering the blessing of rain,
and I am drawn in and leap
above the table

float with you
on the same pink cloud.
We are one heart,
speaking poems that do not rhythm
and bringing bouquet after bouquet
to each other
clasped in the hand of death.

For to love this completely
is to die over and over.
And it is ecstatic,
it is what I want.

So then let the ripping begin,
that ecstatic ripping of fear tissue,
which grew in place,
got locked in place by hours of driving
on the same old roads
with the wrong partners.

For we have found each other,
and our path is unraveling
splendidly. It is a new road,
there is no road really.

At least you are that for me
and I know you would say it
in your way in Spanish perhaps,
with your rich chocolate voice
granting and opening me,
and I am that for you too.

The brightness between us
is so bright
that we read poems
with sunglasses on.
We swirl, in our
ancient-new solar system,
a pink cloud supporting us.

One heart – sacred heart,
an ocean heart with rose petals
and gardenia blossoms
falling around us,

gifting those we love.

Fish School

His hands move before him,
a school of fish darting, weaving
they swim through sea weed, old orange rinds

from fishing boats passing overhead.
I swim with the fish
knowing he's really trying to seduce me
all the time, I see him underwater.

This woman knows the water, I weave in and out
of stories he only alludes to, broken vows,
grown daughters and sons he can never know.
He bleeds for what he threw away.

He could not know I was all the time,
shaking my rattle
doing a dance in honor of his grief
Singing, singing to the ancestors.

I shake my rattle from an old turtle shell
filled with crystals from ant hills, tiny, hard, matching tears
that fall to the ocean bottom, and never dissolve.

I sang while we ate sushi
while he walked me to my car
and gave me a brotherly hug.

I leave him standing alone. Still he could not weep
could not understand why I left, they left,
why the fish swim around him even now.

Wedding Rite

Cutting the cake
we join our hands at the blade
slice through white cake, butter cream,
poppy seeds and raspberry mousseline.

It tastes as good as it looks,
a confectioner's dream
with ribbons of satin white truffle
outside that ruffle,
a gusset of perfection,
that holds every morsel together

Until we've opened the bodice
spoon each other
sighing thank you
thank you.

Sinking My Hands

into hot water
melting the grease away
from dirty dishes
from the blue and white plates
painted with the story of Chinese lovers,

The sky goddess
and the river god
travel over
the half-round bridge
of the Milky Way.

Bubbles, transparent crystal balls,
pop the fantasy my sister spoke
when she gave them to me.
I can still see her face
glowing when I reach through the suds

for a dirty knife
made by stout hands,
forged into a rapier
worthy of succulent
fruit. Raising the glistening

blade, it rings a glass
and sounds far away,
bongs the stainless
steel sink holding
my hands and dishes

eternally without effort
without a thought
just doing what it has been shaped to do,
like the round shoulders
of my Grandmother,

shaped by years of bending
over the sink,
over the Chinese lovers,
clinking a glass
with a silver spoon,

smoothing the surface
of my favorite wooden bowl,
the one for superior salad dressing,
this one passed through my Mother's
kitchen on to me.

My hands fold over
their memories night after night.

Coming Home

You left the lights on for me
no sound, just the hiss of the CD player.
I knew you'd been dancing.

Switching off lights, player,
following my nightly steps
to the back of the house, I hear your gentle snore,

not in bed, but in the guest room on the floor
laying in front of our altar, crowning your head,
your dancing pants are on, one hand slipped inside,
your usual sleeping position.

The exhaustion of work has melted from you,
yet the lines in your face
seem deeper from your long days this week.

I see in the candle light symbols of your life;
red, blue and white cloths under
a feathered man dancing, with the potent irons
of Ogum, a God of Fire,
I see your shells from Puerto Rico, your Taino sun.

I watch your bearded cheeks blow out and suck in
the air, fire, water and earth of the altar
blue and gold veils drape from a shelf above you.

Then I say 'hello' softly, let the words float on your inhale.
You open your eyes, come out of your dream,
you knew it would be me.

'I had to awaken the altar tonight,' you say, and you have.
You danced your prayers for your sons, our families, this crazy world.
I lean over and give you a kiss.
You bury your head in my neck, my breasts.

I lie down with you sharing a pillow
cradling your face
in the glow.

Blue Box of Memories

My sister shipped me a box of memories, sent as I had left it, packed without packing between jars. Opening the blue flaps and scotch tape,

I find glass shards from powdered pigment jars, the culprit phthalocyanine blue bottle, watercolors of all colors, a loose cap of cobalt.

My hands become blue handling blue photos of black Mrs. Tingley from 3rd grade, pale Miss Smith from 2nd, a blushing Greg Green.

Blue letters for sports I'd won still waiting for a sweater I never bought. Blue photos from High School, a brown yearbook now blue.

My blue seventeenth year last Will and Testament written before my near-death, the story of that black storm, my first blue year in college mixed with

Zinc white independence, chrome yellow power learning subjects I didn't know I loved. Ultramarine Blue dance cards, still empty and awkward stacked on top of

Angry orange writing over the War in Vietnam, Mars Red rants from the harm we cause the Earth in drawings with my practiced artist signature.

A blue Kathie Kolwitz book of drawings, blue photos of boyfriends exempt from the draft. A young husband sailing on a boat too far away to remember why I left, or did he leave me?

Baby nieces and nephews, blue newspaper clippings with evidence of my name in print, slides of a friend's hippie wedding by the blue-black pond.

The blue-green of my eyes, hopeful for a day when the blues would disappear. Now I reach back, see her blue face,

say welcome, I am here, thriving on the Pacific coast, greening, greening wild rainbows beyond these blue memories.

Blue Bones

We circled on the beach
with friends who came to wish us well.
Ernesto said a prayer. I held her ashes

in a pine needle and sweet grass basket.
Ernesto held a pale pink rose.
I touched him with her ash. The wind howled and

sea foam spewed over our shoes
"The sea is kissing us," someone said.
He blessed me with her ash.

We walked to the shore. He took
a pinch and I took a pinch. Our fingers barely
fit inside the basket rim.

Waves hit our shoes and we were soaked knee deep.
Our pinches hit my shoes with sea foam and sand.
I was covered in my daughter's tiny bones.
Some green and blue bits colored my white socks.

"Robin's egg blue" I thought.

Take her Yemaya, Take her winds of the West.
Blow and mix her tiny body with the Earth.
Take our baby who blessed us, take the grief from my uterus.

Ernesto threw up his arms in thanks,
I did the same. He turned back.
I stood stock still.

This beach is where I labored two weeks before,
before the pain forced me to let her go,
where I first sobbed her loss.

Now we bring her back to sea and foam,
where she began and never touched the Earth
until now. I prayed to the waters sweet and salt,

and felt the blessing of rain on my red cheeks
my saturated skin, my numb fingers, I turned around.
Two friends stood like centauries of motherhood,

sisters, one a mother four times, me a mother once,
step-mother twice, one a mother not at all, though
a step-mother four times.

I hugged them both long and hard, made a triangle.
I shed what I knew were not the last of my tears
for our baby, Mariluna del Sol. They held me all the way back,

We walked in the sand and rain,
our baby's bones mixed with sand and sea,
her star bone bits in the sea and salt,
her blue bones rest on my shoes.

Collapse

There is a trap door in my chest,
even though I have laid the finest
parquet flooring over it.
A door well hidden
by carpets and lamps, couches,
a foot stool.

Looking so casual, relaxed almost,
sipping a cup of Earl Grey
at a restaurant or a pub, it always happens
in casual conversation with strangers
when it is my turn to speak
and cannot.

There is no latch on the door on the outside
but it swings open again and again inside
and all the furniture
arranged so carefully
tumbles.
There is no way
to stop the falling.

It is that damn skeletal hand that opens it.
Words cannot fit into parquet,
like babies and motherhood
questions that kill such as
Do you have children?
or in consolation,
Why don't you adopt?

Often when hearing them I think;
I can do it,
Just sit here on my couch and pretend.
See the hours I've spent
making the pieces fit back together,
look at the rug woven from my cut hair
stained with blood, laced with salt tears,
look at the lamp

how it makes the room brighter.
But then that latch clicks open
and the falling begins.

All the power goes out
storms demand entry,
there is no end
to falling.

And while the speaker
didn't mean to trip the latch,
it is mine after all,
opens from the inside once again,
I lose all control,
fall every time
wish it weren't happening,
want to be someplace else,
there is nothing to be done.

But feel the silence crack open,
thunderheads burst,
lightening bolts pierce
setting fires,
the endless torture of rain.

There is no
decorative room
no walls to touch
only down and in
and too many days of tears

and remembering your
still tiny body,
your bright daughter's
hand on my shoulder
your love
pouring over me
even now.

Ashes

We threw them into the salty sea and wind,
her tiny bones clung to my socks, my shoes
I could not, would not shake them off.

We turned back from the sea,
from the waves,
from the eternal night.

We pressed our palms
to the wind, blowing us into
horizontal sea spume.

Her heart floats between
stars somewhere,
mine remains in the raging sea,

yours in the eternal night.
Her bones
are blue.

Brave Ones

I admire the mad one
for touching
those shards
hard and cutting.

Who is brave enough
to own the tyrant,
the one who won't let us
sleep, won't let us love?

Who will face the angry one,
who's splintering rage makes joints sore,
resentful to be left mourning years
after death has marked their home?

Who has tried on their dead son's
clothes, just to smell him again?
Walked around in their mother's shoes?
Used Grandma's dinner plates in memoriam?

My heroes feel everything,
leave no fragments alone,
leave no questions
for others answer.

The brave press their palms against the wind
scream with the raging sea
tear streaked and
yes, mad from the breaking.

The sane ones find their brokenness beautiful
they make stained glass from the fragments
hold a thousand autumn leaves to the sun
trace rivers of veins to the sea

They hold themselves hostage and safe
while they rock and rock
to the music of loss
only they can hear.

The Gods are Melting

into each other;
Kwan Yin and White Buffalo Calf Woman,
Kali and Kwan Yin,
Buddah and Jesus,
Amachi and Liberachi,
the eagle and the pigeon,
mouse and rat,
St. Gregory and St. Germain,
Mother Mary and Mother Theresa,
Madonna and Judith,
Sheva and Star Woman,
Xango, the African God of Lightening
and Pan, the God of Earthly delights,

the Mountain and the rain clouds,
rivers and the sea,
rocks and sand,
sand and surf,
stars and sky,
sun and earth,
earth and moon,
moon and woman,
sun and man,
man and woman,
moon and sun,
mind and body,
eyes and ears,
hand and mouth,
you and me.

The Turning

Today on my walk
a woman stands at the end of the road

her back to me, blonde hair streams down beyond her waist,
hands drawn up around her mouth

she seems in shock or awe,
standing before a towering altar of pines.

Perhaps she listens to jazz rising from the stream below.
Perhaps she has found fresh remains of a mountain lion's prey.

Perhaps she has had words with her mate
and what pools around her feet, remnants of ice.

Closing the House

She vacuums
the dust balls
that float with grief
where their bed once stood.

She sweeps over and over
the most tender of memories,
picks out of the carpet
their years of touching -
his body, her hands.

She stands at the window
for the last time
and watches the rain gather
over the mountains.

Winding the vacuum cord
from peg to peg,
she walks across the carpet,
and closes the door
to the empty room
as streaks of sun
break through.

Poem for Jeanine Kalica at 17

Her spirit is moon light
poking out from behind the cloud.
Her belly swelling with fullness
of her broadening light,
waning, thin, then
a silver gate for stars
to pass through.

Grandmother,
bring her over the milky way bridge,
I know she is a shooting star,
red tail flare.
She is coming towards you,
take her in your star fire arms.

Bring her away
to your milky way land
give her a chance to
dance her pain and rage,

let her live fire
and not be scorched
let her fly
and never land.
Earth is too harsh
for those on fire,
Waters sear
freckled skin,
Air enrages
ragged fires.

Take her between
your star-lit palms.
Help her land safely
on her blazing star.

Inscriptions
East Cliff Drive - Santa Cruz

Overlooking The Hook,
sitting on a bench above,
I rest back on a plate
bearing a name,
wonder who she was.

Dedicated to a woman surfer,
a young one from the dates
of her span, I read;
See you on the flip side,
ride out in peace.

As I look towards
the split rail fence
the cliff falls away to
cerulean blue ocean
a clear sky day, as surfers
ride out their dreams.

One young woman
inscribes the waves.
Go, girl, I whisper as she
cuts back again and again.

Shifting my focus, gray letters
on the split-rail emerge
from gray-brown.
Someone tagged,
I'm proud of you.

No street name,
no stylized letters, just
a generous wish to anyone
who needs a lift.

I want to etch back,
...this is how
we get through.

instead I whisper, "Wow, thanks!
me too ... you, whoever
you are."

Reunion

Oh how I have missed you
how I want your touch,
this treble voice falters.

I cannot hear another
line of introduction.
Stop!
When will we
slowly dissolve?

Release this madness
open your waiting palms

inside this well
of longing
turns
an empty pail.

Oh, fill me.

Birth Day

On the day I was born,
some where the sea must have churned
like it does today, ripping and
boiling the sands
shaping and reshaping them.

But I was born landlocked
in deep winter snows,
three weeks late,
reluctant to renter the cold.

I didn't know then
that everything caste to the sea
dissolves
or is taken apart.

Today on the shore
I am wet to my knees,
watching sandpipers run
harbor-bound boats
turn and roll in the waves.

On the beach
I find pieces of bow sprint,
bulbs of bullwhip kelp,
stripes of seed weed and
drift wood washed clean of its bark.

And the waves in the night
left a two foot cliff by the water
weaving long rolls of debris.

Standing in a river, made by rain over night,
sweet water meets salt.
Stones of my past round and flat
suspend between ripples of sand.

    I hurl one into a wave,
a disc for a salty discus thrower.
    One becomes a gift I decide,
so I tuck it into my vest.

    My feet are embedded
on this eroding shore,
nothing unmoving stands long
in this place where
salt and sweet water become one.

    Today I know that salt water shapes the Earth,
and I am happiest here near the sea,
watching the changes,
boiling with possibility.

    Holding on to nothing,
but a rain soaked feather
I stand where

    Two bodies of water,
a third of air, open me
to the carving.

    On this day of my birth
I can say without reservation

    I have learned to sail!

Work Week

Every weekday morning,
though you say good morning
when you walk to the shower,
you are already in that meeting
which doesn't start 'til 9.

You were really here all weekend
which makes Mondays so vacant,
even though we speak
while we make breakfast
you are miles down the road.

Then the surprise, you turn back to
kiss me good-bye,
racing back for a brief peck,
a little squeeze.

Just as suddenly you are
no where to be seen
driving off to catch up with your mind
that left ahead of you.

Pacheco Pass

Reins of wires loop
across golden hills
to water dammed, surging,
funneled to rotating turbines.

Our Ford truck moves towards
another source,
sun setting beyond felted hills
lined with furrows of trees
folded dales where rivulets flow
into the San Luis Reservoir.

We cross the dam, a four-lane highway.
On the left, acres of water,
on the right, steep hills hide us
cool in the long shadows, now blazing sun,
now shade again.

Traveling westward and up
horses cluster among
long tree shapes under trees
spot the hillsides with dark green
leaves, dark gray stretching,
longer, longer, blending with each other

joining the east side of the hill
pulling blue shade across the ridge
blanketing everything in cool darkness
as the sun sinks behind Hollister, Gilroy,
now the Pacific rim of the Monterey Bay.

Encounter

When I encounter you,
a response is necessary
or we blow apart
just like photons and neutrons
in a strong or weak nuclear interaction.

We are not who we were before the encounter
and not who we have been after.

Everything has to change
and now we are seeking a way through
born from a strengthening identity with light
born from this flap and swoop of black holes
of this interaction, a convening, a rejoining,

now we spin off in our own directions
discovering something entirely new.

Dream of the Last Tapestry

We became cubist
renderings. Our tap-
estry of herons by
the pond dissolved.
Two faces, those
threads of love be-
tween us, cut away.

We became habits
for the other. Strain
of death fractured our
resolve. I am not your
white oppressor. You
are not my slave master.
I slipped off your leash.

Just as these lines are finished

the miracle of forty geese

land on this very

pond.

Iowa River 500 Year Flood Blues

Up stream was
  every where around them.
Behind the houses
      the park became a home
           for wetland birds.

Someone erected a sign
'neighborhood wide -
wet carpet sale'.
Everyone paddled over
for a laugh.

Nan spent
     her summer
  in a canoe,
ferrying her family
     from the second floor
of their split level,
     to the base of the hill
on the next block.

Thick basement mud
     drowned Nicky's snake.
The dog and two cats
     spent their summer
at the pound,
     no dry place to pee,
no lawn left to throw a Frisbee,

Everything from downstairs
was stacked upstairs
 no place to eat,
     or read a book.
Raw sewage everywhere,
soaked their ruined drywall.

Receding waters beached canoes,
and rubber ducks tied
to the mailbox, remind us
      months after
 why the park still
looks like a
      moon scape.

Fences

Two horses, separated
by a barbed-wire fence,
  make a lovely oval
  from the chest up.

They lick each other's wounds
  at the place on the other
    where the fences
    make them stop.

Touching Center

Lying in lines of sunlight
    I watch your eyes
        trace me in the long grass.

I have taken in cells of love
    from your finger tips,
        those infernal sparks,
and placed them in my wounds
    to cauterize the scars.

Your persistent touches
    pull me out of self-burning,
        bring me into the twentieth century,
    let me rest on Halloween
        in the arms
        of Christ.

Night may come again,
    but the sparks will not fade,
        burning edges of the fire ball
    healing the wounds of centuries
        I am bound to dissolves.

I carry your night lantern
    into my day,
        your kisses like fireflies
            lighting my path,
    tiny bolts of lightening
        gently touching me.

A Perfect Flight

For my Father at 99

If I could give you words as a gift
they would be,
you are enough.
The time of proving yourself is past.

If I could share with you my observation
of a life well lived   I would say,
you are the thunder and the rain
and after the storm   the stained-glass sun.

If I could sit with you by the lake
lace my arm through yours
as we watch the geese glide away
I would say to you,

Pop, look how the geese
practice their formation over and over
how they teach their young the art
of family moving together.

When they have accomplished
their rehearsals   we would see them
take a running flap
and an awkward pounding of wing

To become
one with the dawn
one with a distant
star.

Finding Each Other

How can I speak
about the way two streams
fall from the same mountain,
meet, mix and flow together.

Their union depends on
the minerals in those hills,
soft places,
where the land
gives way
to the persistent trickle
of nourishment
for spawning fishes.

Renewal occurs
in the cycle of evaporation
falling from clouds,
hiding this blue hope
we open to on sunny days.

One thing I know,
you can't figure out the finding.
It is only as natural
as an earthquake,
or as a heron
stretching her wings,
over a lagoon.

In a pool of clouds
she finds her mate
standing there
looking through her reflection,
taking what comes to him.

They share the familiar;
the same source
flowing from the river.
They share safe places
and hunting grottos.

Their strength
is the way
they are
simply themselves,
lifting off
to find
their place
above the river,

nesting
on a broad fan of pine,
on the back
of the same
ever changing
mountain.

Raven Man

The Ravens hang around him waiting.
He knows they are there.
He asks me what they are trying to say.

Suddenly I see them
one perched on each shoulder
ready to lift him up.
Another at his back
to stop him in his tracks.

A fourth laying over his head
beak on his forehead
wings over his shoulders
to indicate this warriors
last dance.

They speak to me
in a chorus;

Only when he is ready,
only when he decides.
His fight is over,
they await his final flight.

I am the bearer
of this message to him.
He throws his head back
smiles and with a 'no' in his voice
 he caws;

I know! I know! They'll just take me!
Don't you worry your pretty head.
Somehow I am the one broken
from his news.

He jumps up with stick thin raven legs.
 Did I show you my new toy?

He is glowering at me now.
It is a sword,
jagged edge on one side,
razor sharp on the other.
It scares me, though I sit firm.

Now he flaps his arms
with the sword
telling me of a flock
that circled him
on the beach in Mexico.

Then he sheaths his sword
and runs to his room.
Off his altar he takes his prize
creation. It is a red blown glass

womb that he made himself.
A silver lead-glass rim around its mouth
and elegant drip is suspended in mid-air
pointing up

He hands it to me. Smoke it with
sage before you use it.

I had always wanted one of his glass
pieces. He couldn't make them anymore.
I think he just asked me
to pray for him.

Then he flaps to the kitchen.
Let me show you what keeps me alive.
It is a tea concoction he makes with
no shortness of chili peppers.

I drink this all day!
He chortles again.

I sip it and choke.
A ravens brew!
I say with a smile.
He grins, eyes dancing.

He flies around the room,
His heart is on fire.
His body falling apart
from Vietnam, agent orange,

His own phoenix
exploding.

For Kathleen

The last time I saw her
she was skin and bones
walking outside her house
with her baby niece sleeping
in a carriage.

I laid the flowers I brought
down next to her front door
behind the tall green
bamboo hedge,

And we walked up
and down the block,
up and down the block
ever so slowly.

She told me with her
radiant smile of her story
its link to her cancer
that was eating her up,

What she had to do
to speak her truth for the sake
of everyone. How this helped
her let go of the disease.

I said nothing, just listened
and heard her story,
held it as a delicate flower
she was offering.

We walked up and down
and up and down
she finally said, 'Oh now
I went and told you
the whole thing!'

As though
she hadn't meant to
but had anyway.

Back at her front door
we hugged each other,
laughed about the way
we humans are.

Brave
For Stan Rushworth

He stood at the podium
holding on to it
to steady his palsied shaking

Then, like a Sundancer,
he bore his chest to be pierced
chanting his poem-prayer to the Earth,
for us to wake up to her sacred body.

As the elder medicine man
he called in wind, earth, fire, water,
he invoked the very powers as it rained
gently outside in response.

He called out to all of us, she is yours
to care for

then he said, somewhere in the chanting
to the young ones:
She is your mother too.
Take hold.

Then he closed his eyes as he read the incantation
his spirit hand brushing over her muddy body,
he placed her markings on his own face
over his brow, on his cheeks, a line on his chin.

He ended the way he started, releasing the four
directions, giving thanks for the fire, earth, water, air,
calling to wind.

As he finished he stood at the podium firmly, not shaking,
eyes closed, humming her praise,
as though it was his last message to us,
wings sprouting from his arms to rise.

The Animal Man

He moves like a cat
agile, on fire
walking through any gate
like he belongs there.

Like something wild
he marks his territory
stands with his pride,
and savors everything
intensely.

A master of the big cats,
falcon and eagle,
the black wolf with
wild yellow eyes,

He is the animal man
who shares his world
with a privileged few,
and burns every ember
to ash.

Bird Memories

Seven poets discuss

the lifting off into air

    hang-gliding

sitting together in silence

all of us sense the rush.

One speaks in reverie

    of weightlessness.

Yet we all seem to remember

something way back,

    of actually being a bird

leaving the nest

    wings open

        the rise.

Lost and Found
Inspired by David Wagoner's poem 'Lost'

I have been lost in a forest.

Once while riding in a car
with a man I loved,
we hit a cat.
It wasn't black,
but it tugged at my belly
when it got caught under the wheels
just the same.

Another time, while crossing the desert,
I felt icicles on my sun burnt chin
and played with them
just to be sure I could still feel.

On and on, my partner and I skied
into the woods, so far away from the trail
that my legs got wobbly.
As it grew dark,
we found a cabin.
"We could make a home here," he said.
Thank God, I got rescued by the ski patrol.

This time I don't want to kill another cat,
or get lost in the desert,
or get rescued by anyone,
I only want to feel my own feelings
and breath the air from pine trees
and dance naked on the beach,
if I want to,
just because I am.

Sliver of Anger

A crystal chip under the skin
looks like glass
so fine no one knows it's there,
except you,
"A little chip," you say.

I have a right to speak up
to speak out
to get even
to get angry
to answer the phone
or not
to shout my name.

Perhaps its my star ship
chip
star chip
chip of fools
chart of stars
chart of chips

maybe it's another clue.

Etheriate

Tonight you are invisible,
come through the walls
      on your own, uninvited.

Tonight I am weak
don't have the heart to kick you out
I want you here   regardless
of my resistance.
We curl and uncurl for hours.

You are a crow, an owl,
      a cat silent yet felt.

Tonight is an infusion, a territory,
an explosion.
Hand on hand on bodies.
How singular the beaten
tapestry night.
Feathers fly in sleepless pillow beating.

The actions of the day are an
unwound wing,
How is it you are here and not here?
Did I pull you in
or have you come again
over my   protestations?

You come through my dreams
we discuss everything.
You are still here by morning.
As you get up and walk through and   away
you say: I will see you later.

I don't believe you, can't believe you
The scent of you is still in my bed
Your invisibility lingers
all morning.

Love Clouds

We swirl in a cloud.
Streams belong to bigger streams,
belonging to what is
all around us.

Our thoughts
are out in front of us
laying in patterns,
our futures.
Everything is malleable,
constantly changing.

This pink cloud we are in
hooks into another
and the swirls get bigger
and form
more patterns of weather.

The swirls branch
and branch
into new streams
washing
everything
clean.

I Go My Own Way
for David Whyte

I was expecting to be done with you,
yet standing together a final time
seems impossible.

Poetry has cut me closer to you
than I thought likely
and your generous praise
and gifts of the soul leave me
speechless.

So here we stand. I am
reading poems
between the lines on your face,
not able to say
"Thank you"
in its full measure,
not able to utter
another goodbye.

You and your poems
have been the cake of pearls
I have feasted on
all this time
each bite another jewel.

In your irascible humility
you remind us all that it is
something bigger than our
two hands folded together,
it is nothing anyone can grasp.

Yet, in your eyes
and around your mouth
a kind of light flickers,
a flippant knowing

that, whether we know it or not,
poetry will always
bring us
face to face again.

After Candlemas

A full moon casts blue light on the snow,
violet and green, an aurora borealis
on the earth at 20 below.

Here in a frozen field the rendezvous,
under a blanket of snow,
the earth and night sky come together
burst, and fade with color-light,
silent, deep surrender.

God Parents
for Paul and Bretta

Like silk ribbons
of pale blue, gold
and magenta,

Softer than silk,
these streams
thrum through

The gentle touch of our hands
this child that sleeps
the full length of my body

As the full moon lights us
through the window
of the van
on a long ride home.

Ode to Hatsy

Something secret passed between us,
too precious to speak about,
when you gave my hand a squeeze
or offered delectables
from your kitchen.

We listened for the secret,
during lacing hours
of conversation,
through a poem, or
a silver tea pot,
a hand made spoon of horn,
the maker or user
imprint embedded.
Then you gave the story,
the heirloom,
that connected us,
something from the past
to pass on.

It was both the object
and the essence you
handled so carefully,
"touching the hand that
touched," you would say.
And we knew while
these moments passed
they were dear,
slipping into our top
memory drawer.

Yes, it was the essence
of that nectar,
      we sipped together
in your kitchen,
this moment and the next,
 pearl after pearl.

Trick or Treat

Clear umbrellas
open in the rain
make yellow maples
Monet-esque.

Black umbrella boarder
frames yellow trees
and children,
now a Mary Cassatt.

A wet belly dancer
skids towards her
last performance
ala Tolouse La Trec.

Jodell

Your red hair flares
a torch of feeling floods
your cheeks.
You are flush with change,
radiant with colors of these
fluttering green blinds
open to the sun.

Cape of Ulysses

They say he stuffed Mullein leaves
in his underwear
to protect from those sirens.
He ordered his men to do the same,

and had them press those soft
leaves into their ears,
then apply wax,
to seal against their song.

He had his men sew him a cape
of Mullein leaves then strap him
to the mast. Only Ulysses' ears were open
to listen to their seductive choir

and his binds would protect him from those whispers
and sighs from their groans and gyrations
from going mad,
from turning his ship into the rocks.

Poor Ulysses. What of the night?
Did you really think
you could stop any hot-blooded Siren
from seeping into your dreams?

A Cold Promise

She takes my money for the mammogram.
The first one this morning,
        but I still have to wait
        for the technician
    to finish dipping the films
of other women's breasts.

I made myself a promise
        after my sister sent an article
written about
her breast cancer,
the same year as my divorce,
        what cataclysmic constellations
whirled in the cosmos then?

The article told
        of what she went through,
what she goes through everyday since,
How she stepped through the door that said
        `this moment is your life,
there may be no other.'

It's time to wake up
get your life checked
I walk into the cold room.
The technician says
        "Step up to the machine please."

Baby Porcupine

Today she paints her toes
      sitting in the sun.
Her wounds are healing,
        she has shed the old patching of armor
            that used to protect her.

Instead she grows retractable quills,
        ones that extend if you tread upon her.
Yet her underbelly is still tender
      no one can touch her,
          except perhaps another porcupine.

Each quill has a tiny feather on it,
      some are painted defiantly healing.
The feathers quiver in the wind
      foretelling storms, jogging things loose.

They shake a little
      when she dances
           across the telephone wires.

No Bread

His head is bobbing and weaving
        to the rhythms of traffic.
Each car dives the mice in his mind
        on wheels spinning.

No one knows how he got here,
           a journey
       as tattered as his clothes.

Echoes from those mice stir me.
        Unsavory smells stick to my shoes
              like gum. Behind his thin face
those mice grind flour
        which trails behind him.

Birds peck and pick up
        the grains leading back to the time
              when everything tumbled.
The trail from yesterday, gone.

Who is baking bread for him?
        No one slices a hot loaf,
              sips tea with him
                      in a warm kitchen.

The wind blows. Do not
        dust him away like the flour.
What storm blew his house down?

The sun of the city burns,
        the night turns cold and cutting.
Where does this man go
        without a loaf of bread?

Bombs over Baghdad - 1991

The father's eye explodes over Baghdad
mixing with the Tigris and Euphrates.
Those same waters where oil
spills like the blood of Iraqi generations
where men, blind with greed,
sell the Earth's blood
raping the fertile crescent,
fertile no more.

Over the cradle of civilization
some fathers without sight
drop bombs on other's children
and do not see that kill their own.
Other parents will not return
to see their children or read them stories
or tuck them in at night.

Where are the leaders, men and women,
who paint a vision for our children
and teach about the fertile crescent
and tell stories of ancestors.
What is civilization when in bomb shelters,
children learn only survival without fathers
or mothers,
without vision?

Reverberation
Part I - 02-11-11

Songs oscillate from building to building in Cairo's epicenter
in Tahrir "Liberation" Square. Baste, her black fur twitching,
stands up to listen to the revelry, sauntering through this new Egypt.
Her cousin, the Sphinx, shakes off the crown of the pharaoh
and licks his paw in contentment. He no longer needs to sit guard
outside Giza. He and cousin Baste have waited five millennia
for people to take charge of their lives. Today the people send out
a shock wave felt on the tips of the fur of all harmonious cats.
Baste, as the keeper of harmony, hearth, protection, peace,
stretches her long back as a wave, a cheer, a sonic boom
echoes along the Nile to the Tigris and Euphrates around the world
as the great cats launch off into the desert—to exert freedom.

Part II - 02-11-12

This was harder than anyone thought. Yet, there is no turning back.
What the cats were waiting for, has not come easily. Think of any
Revolution, all have risen to the people's demands.
Bloodshed is so hard to avoid after any good or bad king.
Call on Baste.
She walks between worlds
with answers to the riddles the Sphinx holds.
She says: Sharing power opens
an elusive way, inconceivable to power mongrels—empower all
to build their own futures—engaging the heart.
Bring peace through everyone working
together for food on all tables. Employ those desert cats.

Part III - 08-14-2013

Don't pick up that gun. It does not help extend your member. Become a falcon flying over. Better yet, become the dung beetle and wait until the time for peace becomes right again.
See with the eyes in your chest, the only ones that see globally. Remember you are eternal. Align yourself with the Milky Way. Let the women have their way. You cannot do this without them. They belong to the secret order of cats. Women know subversive integrity. Don't let your dog feel ashamed. We have all been waiting for the taste of this sweet ripe date.

Lanterns

Spindrift dusts my face
I thank Mother Ocean
for your kisses.

Sun arrives after days of rain
and invites me
to watch waves undulate.

Your warmth still with me
from yesterday, tiny love lanterns
float through me,

with a bell on each lantern
the harmony we play together
is a resonant chorus-

a song
I haven't heard
before.

Succulent Art Collection

I collect you, works of art,
lovers of my past.
One sculpture
another painting,
memories, impressions,
    savory or hard.

Each one of you has
quirks and diatribes.
One gathers me like a weaver
into his arms.
Another spreads me like
    tubes of bright oily colors.

I have never regretted my lovers
being the colors, the flavors they are,
delicious succulent morsels
of divine fruit.
I am delicious too,
    sensuous mango.

Taste my flavors, let me
touch your lovely
passion apples.
I feel you ripple
take in your sweetness,
dissolve you,
    salt in sea.

I bite you tenderly
this mouth absorbing your flavors
morsels of vanilla, raspberry
sushi, chocolate, cream, tangerine.
Lick and savor me,
    let my juices flow.

Bartering at the Border

If I hide you in my purse
will they take you away
 like the whale bones,
like confiscated plants,
like marijuana kilos
or will they send you back
to your mother and father,
        to a pimp?

Who loves you more than anything?
Will you ever have a chance to thrive?
Your whining voice doesn't tell me
what I want to hear
nor your hair streaked with rain,
face wet with tears.

Stop begging me, stop begging,
I can not give you something for nothing,
I can not give
I can not give a peso,

You brand me
with your empty hands
your hollow eyes,
your thin
yellow serape.

Napping with Minka

I rest with my cat
on my torso.
She leaves one paw
on the amber bobble
that hangs from my neck.

Claws flex and retract,
one eye closed
one eye watching me
for a twitch or a smile.

She rests expectant
ready to play,
ready to sleep,
waiting for my next breath
to make up her mind.

Big Birds

Dipping into the back
of ships
Swedish cranes unload
cargo, these

mechanical storks, look like
birds, their glass bulbs
full of water. They
drink then rise and drink again
at the edge of the harbor.

Stone Circles

Stark naked at forty-eight,
I raise my arms in circles, like the waves,
one then the other then I lift my leg
and see my perfect shadow,

nipples, one then the other,
bushy mound, full belly
my thighs and legs,
my feet and pointed toes.

I have done my ritual dance to the Gods.
take my honoring bow to the elements,
and turn to find a stone duplicate of
my frozen scapula there.

I have danced it out of me.
I make an offering of my hair
pick up the shale shoulder blade,
with cracks running through it, fault lines,
where I blamed myself for everything.

It is the shoulder where
I picked up the weight of the world,
turned over every stone in my path
the shoulder where I counted every penny.

I carry it around, stroke it
and remember everything that made it tight,
instead of marking moments,

now and now and now.

At the core, it is the ligament that connects
the shoulder blade to the collar bone,
that has hardened into metal.

Dancing has altered the metal
to bend, soften, dissolve,
It has melted here on the sea edge.

Breaking the slab along the fault lines,
I celebrate the cracks and
throw it against the cliffs
return it to the sand and tides.

Circles of arms take in secluded circle of beach,
stretch legs take a giant stance, a pirouette.
In waves and bends,
my body becomes an osprey.

Last Massage

A man with a hole in his face
tells me he's getting better
as he lies down
for the last time on my table.

My hands, move like quicksilver
to his shoulders.
He bares his neck to me as if he
were ready for me to slice it and
offers his tightness bravely,
so I may knead out the tender places.

A man, already in pain from wild cells
gone mad in his head,
having taken an eye and bits of bone,
still holds a hopeful glance with the other,
and offers me a chance to witness
the wounded shoulder he barters with
for these last precious days.

This man lets me rock his shoulder loose
from its moorings.
Waves of sadness wash over me.
Behind his heart, a cord is strung
so tight, I pluck it
and hear his final tense notes.

I feel as though, in prying loose
the shoulder from his back, I am now
on death's side teasing him to surrender.

Having lost my courage,
I can do no more,
and gently tell him so.
He looks at me a long time,
searching my face for clues,
looking for another route home.

As he leaves, he embraces me for a moment,
says goodbye with one of those final notes.
He has announced his surrender,
I have not cheated him.

But I stand in a puddle of everything
in my day which does not matter.

We both know a terrible and beautiful secret.

Shades Apart

Last night, red petals
of a double-headed rose

swirled like two clouds
a shade apart.

Today my hairdresser
told of the Guatemalan

found in the parking lot
hanging from a eucalyptus tree,

about the time we blossomed together
skin to skin

silence engulfed us like silken fog
like the mist around the hanging man

who we didn't know
we didn't know he died about that time
we hadn't heard about him yet.

Tonight we lay in the fog,
not touching

but touched by the same one,
the one who walks now with the Guatemalan.

And we opened together
like the double-headed rose.

Cat Time

Raccoons steal cherries from the trees.
Their large eyes glow in the dark, while
rain pounds on the roof,
splatters on broad fig leaves and
my bedroom window.

Inside, my Minka rests on my belly,
purring and humming her contentment.
She cares nothing of stalking racoons, or
my impending move away from here.

She loves to sleep upside down,
I stroke her chin with tenderness.
I swear she is smiling.
Minka always gets me in tune
with cat time,
perhaps the true rhythm of the day.

Her purr brings me into the moment,
and she reminds me every second
that nothing is as important
as I make it.

CARRION HUNTERS

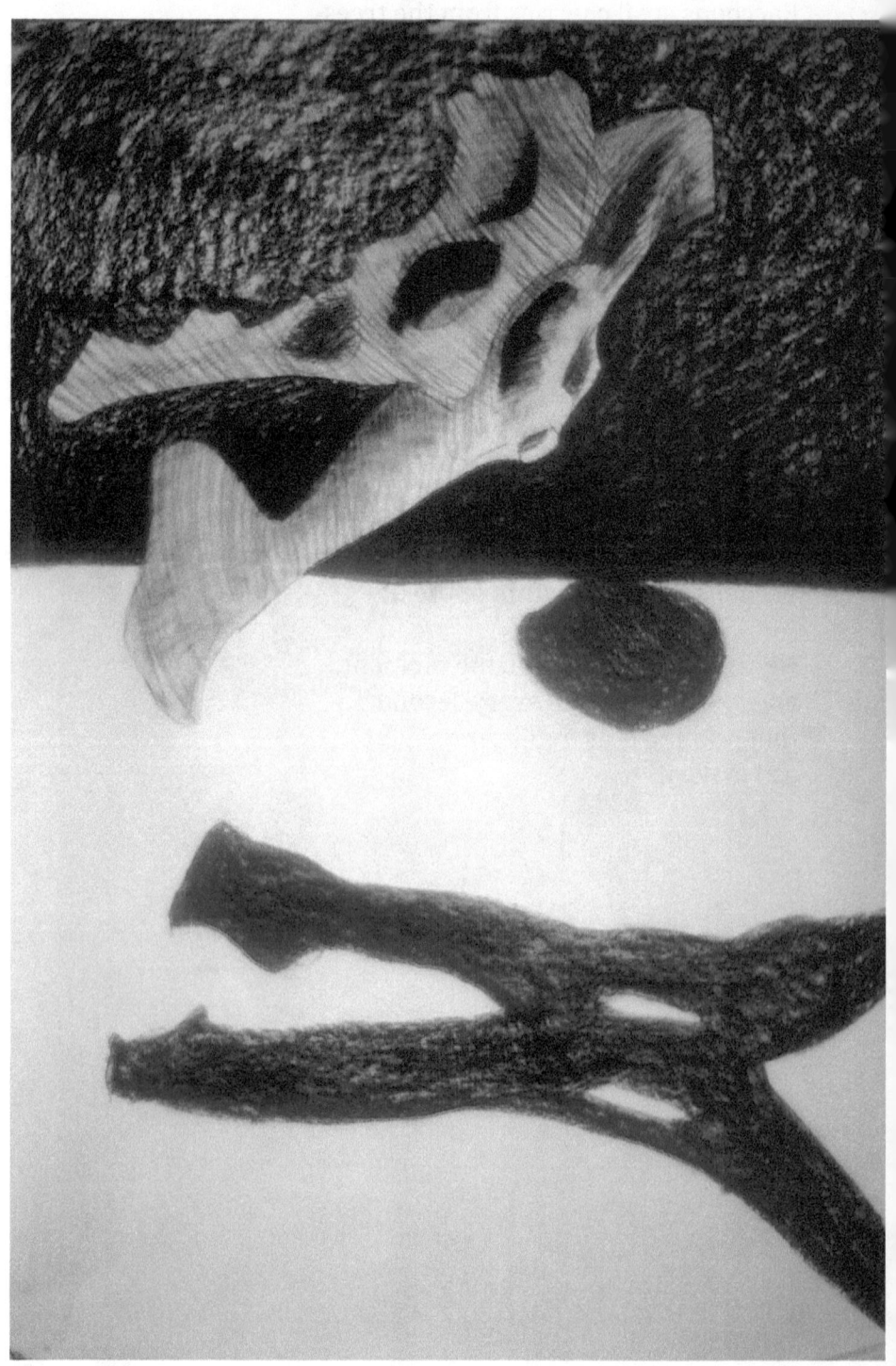

Prow to Bow

Silky rattlesnake grass, hulls
shake into my hand.
Tiny boats
cup into each other,
their seeds tucked
into the prow.

Summer heat dries them.
Wind shakes loose
tiny vessels
to sail into unknown harbors.

Some fall into deep grass,
others sink in wooded glens,
still others sail down
unmarked streams
to chart their passage home.

Pond Lily

I saw you first in late spring
floating in our Waterloo pond
in cool mud
stems rise and float.

Your leafy tongue
curls in
breaking it's tip first
above the surface
to bend, settle, float.

A broad open hand
stretches wide
to receive the sun.

The wax of your leaves
coats you,
your chlorophyll
sends signals
down to the tight bud fist
wending its way up to the surface
following your snaking stem.

A child bud rises above your parental leaf
opens on it's way to settling down on
your green palm cup.

All summer we see you,
White, pink and yellow
skirts a twirl in Oak shade.

You lilies are born like us
in a tangle of other stems
each rising uniquely
to flower from soil.

At summer's end
you turn down again
rain burning yellow holes
through green rafts.

But the sight
of what took all of May and June
to emerge
lasts even after the first frost,
after the ice seals you in
your winter tomb.
Then the early rain
melts the ice as it
pelts you in Autumn.

Dead leaves drift
towards the dam
fall to the bottom
join the mud of your ancestors.

In winter lilies withdraw
as sap into tree
their bulbous roots

hold
white messages
from a lost child,

as ice breaks up
warms pond waters
in sun you rise again

bring your children
to drink rain, and
greet their own
resurrection bloom.

I-90 Pit Stop

Walk in thick June wheat grass
waist high, soft, heavenly
mid-western green waves.

I am Mary Magdalene, Jesus,
trucks blowning by
just three yards from paradise.

Raspberry

Red nugget
tiny sacks of sweet juice
cotton stalk
you are full summer swollen.
I pluck then pop you
between my ready puckered lips,
roll you between
tongue and roof of mouth,
burst of joy.

Field Hands

Broad hands make tortillas
before dawn for the field hand's lunch.
Workers pick strawberries, trim fruit trees,
work before rush hour to past rush hour everyday,
shade only under trees in orchards or alongside of trucks
where hands meet earth to rest
where wild cannea lilies line the edges
of fields and grow in torches.

Hummingbird

buzzes the strange flower
of your red ear
when he flies past
your head
to drink
a dose of nectar
sucking sweetness
from the bottle brush flower.

Babies and Buckeyes

For Jensen and Nico, cousins born eight days apart.

Sing of the Buckeye seedlings sprouting
under a Cayote bush on Mt. Diablo.
On the forest floor, leaves,
green and tender, bend without breaking
under gentle touch.

I wait for these sprouts emergence.
I bend my ear to them,
listen to the hum of their stems
as they push through moist loam
after the rains.

Their spirits are rejoicing. They come
as their ancestors came. Their tiny community
sings together in joyful harmonies
under their parent trees who drape
over them opening new flowers.

I thank them for coming into this wild place.

I sing for Jensen and Nico born this month.
They join the throng of their family lines.
Their parents, once rebels, rejoice
as their ancestors rejoiced, and drape
over their newborns, open as flowers.

I thank them for coming into this place, wild.

Sing for Babies and Buckeyes as they enter the world,
whether the president is black or white,
whether there are wars or famine,
they come when there is money
and when there is none.

They enter the world to be in it.

Born at home or in hospitals, under trees,
in stables, apartments or mansions,
their entrance is a new beginning for everyone.
Babies or Buckeyes arrive
into the same blanket of welcome.

I sing this song to birth.

Mother of Pearl Moon

Suspended in mist
plump and pregnant
face is veiled
your power of gentleness
sways tides.

Carrion Hunters

We drive along way,
until farms spring up
and fences run along the road
dividing field from cattle.

My mother drives,
while I scout,
it feels slightly illegal.

"You will spot their dark round heads
bobbing."
"There," she stops, I fly out of the car
with snipers in hand
a long branch bends towards the ground
woven into the fence
tendrils with curled leaves
and blue-black balls of fruit
bob on slender stems.

This is the prize
named for the odor they emit
when they flower, Carrion Weed,
dead carcasses of rotting flesh,
the odor gone by autumn,
hungry bees have done their work,

these vines hold a graceful fascination
a branch to branch thoughts,
blue heads against white walls,
tendrils spiraling out
dried leave all but removed
in a careful plucking ceremony,
the stem hard and bare
as bone arching.

Two Autumns

Autumn comes like this on the west coast:
bright sun turns dusty,
plants on the side of the road covered
in pale ochre, horsetail skeletons break in two.
Autumn comes with
ferns and raspberries, redwood, and ivy,
all a shade dryer, leaves a pale versions
of their summer vitality.

Here, no maples torch around streams
and blue pearl lakes as in Minnesota,
no red oaks announce the end of Illinois summer.
No one runs from their house saying, "Look!
See how the flames of autumn turn and fall,
how dark thunderheads bring colors out,
see ferns turn to tongues of yellow, sumac ablaze!"

Instead, California mist mingles around redwoods
winter rains seem to never come,
crisp leaves kindle a warning as
infernos rage farther south,
smoke hangs over the Monterey Bay,
and all the while in both lands
we feel the flames of change
inside us.

Casa Blancas
Lily Hypatha

Lily's are seeding.
Black beads dot
their four-fingered pods
to neat green folds.
Opening slowly in cool weather
in this heat
they pop their quatrefoil cage.
Seeds scatter on the sidewalk
clover or
palm of my hand.

One morning I found...

Four perfect rose buds left
one after the other over a mile hike
after the garbage truck
tipped its loads.

Dark red, barely open, scent lingers.
Then I see all are
moldy at the center.

All are narrowed and withered at the neck
bent heads, clogged stems
died as buds

petals still moist
heads droop from heat
scattered on neighborhood streets.

Four roses, three houses
one summer walk.

Last Tilling

Along the fields, wheat grasses bob with
transparent pods back lit
 by early afternoon sun.

Tiny lanterns hold a thousand
Chinese paper memories
held over carriages of ancient landlords.

Bleached grass left from last year, tiny pods
wave in bunches and whip seeds over
opened furrows of newly tilled soil.

Wheat-like grasses, fully ripe in late spring
reddish spikes and green buds veiled
flip and twist in the wind,

Rattling a shimmering wave
long grasses throw a sheen
over the ocean of empty lanterns.

By a split furrow, Rattlesnake Grass line the field
where the farmer has one more season
of tilling before more buildings encroach

Bulldozers peal the top soil back
make little red flag markers fly up and twist back
to clear foundations for corporate profits

Never will seedlings again fall in furrows
waiting for rain
and twist in ripeness under the summer heat.

How Callas were Made

This abundant swirling flower
follows the line of an old Flamenco artist's
last dance.

It was her slow spiral turn, that he loved,
the backwards hand across her face
on the way up to him
her spiral arms turning her torso
she is twenty again as her
satin shoulder is caressed on the way up,
her finger flair beyond her head,
her eyes move from the earth,
twisting counter-clockwise
her head snaps up to him
eyes fixed
on the sun.

Callas

Daunting spirals
      curves of white crepe
                      gateway
              yellow dab
     stems of pale green
  the sea is caught in your
downward gaze,
oceans surge up from
   deep recesses.
From where do you come?
Coils of surprise
              flat panes of care
       cast up and out of the bounty
   you bring to my garden,
     our table
        One twist and I am gone
                wandering
                        down your hollow
                                veils.

Wish

for Nan

                              If
                              I
                           could
                           send you
                                       a trail
                                        of pink
                                              yellow
                                       white
                           I would
                           send
                           calla
                                  lilies.
                     Tender edges
                       spiraling up
                 one continuous fold
           lips open for song or
            praise, curl again
         rise to a point
     hook air, draw a most
     surprising line
     against green
     leaf pallets
      Black earth
      Purple sky.
       I would send
                    you
                this most
                  elegant flower
                         more leaf than
                           petal, the cup
                    holds dew and dreams
                     yellow stamen licking air,
                    peeking out of spiral arms,
                     perhaps not arms but
                     hands folding together
                       holding a whisper,
                              a prayer.

Calla

Veins
of light
ribs of a ship,
You breach with petals for fins
Curl of whale tail bending backwards
into the water, flipping over itself. Yet
the deep silence of this wave you display
straddles the defiant and the Buddha in one breath
oh that seductive curl of flesh, at the culmination
of your curves. My life hangs on the tip and rocks.
I imagine I can climb up then into the slide of slides
down into the yellow dust and stalk, I am yellow,
a bee, deep in your channels and caverns.
Climbing up is not as easy,
I laugh my self silly,
slide down
and drown
in your
luxurious
spirals.

Morning Feed

It is so easy to fill the wooden bird bowl with seeds,
water roses, go from sweet basil
to oregano plants, from sunflower to lemon tree.
To find the hummingbird feeder empty,
because the woodpeckers have been suckling
as well as the hummers.

Too big for the feeder they hang on with black stick feet
on the too small perch, flap and squawk a rattle cry,
red shock of head feathers matches the red liquid they suckled.

No one would believe the comedy. To see them as big as the feeder,
the sweetness only tasted briefly between bitter pecks of their acorn
search. then to the seed bowl,

if the squirrels aren't their first. Few birds confront squirrels, Except
the sparrows who wait and twitter on the iron rail. They chirp, flip
their tails take what is found, fallen or tossed aside.

Chasing the squirrels from the feeder for the hundredth time, I turn
to watch the sparrows come in quickly, waste no time, they come for
a short breakfast meeting. Children of the trees, tiny, playful, curious,
holding their own

with the huge shy band-tailed pigeons. Once I am out of sight, this
flock of pinkish-gray fowl descend like a dream. They gather, with
a few guards, a few picking up around the edges. But most, ten or
twelve, come tightly around the bowl.

Too scared and shy to be seen, its a convention once they are here.
Balancing together on the rim, the slightest sound startles, lifts them
like a gray cloud, an aberration, a miracle. They fly with one mind to
the nearest redwood.

It is the jays turn next. They light on the rail, near the bowl or on the wooden deck. Ink dipped stellar jays, gray and blue scrub jays, they come with their adolescent children to teach them to feed themselves.

Then breakfast for me until I hear the water running outside from the bucket, overflowing, and disturb the birds again, except the hummers, who ignore me, fight their own battles, chirp and buzz. One races close to my head when I bend to grab the hose.

As I straighten my back, she quickly, in midair, stops. Tiny wings a blur, just to look, "hello" she seems to say, and dashes off to play or attach its mate like two ace fighter pilots, darting and racing to the feeder.

It is so easy to spend the morning like this, watering plants watching birds, gazing over the mountains, where they live, where I live, tucked into nests.

Breakfast
for Maggie

Eyes follow a pair of stellar jays
as they feed in the morning
how they
squawk to the
squirrels warning them to move away
how the turtle doves come
to the bath left for them
flipping their gray plumage
into a blur
and the sparrow
hop-flies to seed
spread out,

How the titmouse
is so fierce and tiny.
How they share
the abundant seed feast.
How the young Robin,
still acquiring its full plumage,
shakes and pecks

as a tree leans in,
--a feathered plume in and of itself--
this giant Madrone,
ancient, hollow in spots,
still green,
blossoms bursting,
shades the seed-feast.

My forest family comes in to
echo the world to me then
twitter away to
defend their wild territories.

How their sweetness
is soaked in
how the day begins
with a cacophony
of bright song
lyrics.

El Flamboyán

Flaming canopy
Bright orange orchids
sister to Birds of Paradise
you cluster brightly
to lay your fiery cheek
against a hazy sky.

Black trunk and a few
fans of green
cool your burning flowers

Scattered beneath you in the grass
your orange blossoms
blow across
the road,
are caught
along foot paths
making trails of fire.

Crack, Bang, Boom

How those bright streaks
startled me in the night.
Flash after flash I lay awake
felt safer for their display.
In my childhood home, I sat in
the window seat, my nighty pulled
over my knees, and looked out to the
street through oak leaves, giant
hands, waving wildly.

>How the rain pelted, those cracks shook the house
>Flashes of faces and animal forms appeared in the tree branches
>I loved how my younger sister was scared and
>I was brave, the electricity in my veins
>the fierce laughter of god

Rip Van Winkle
is bowling up there, my grandpa would say
Steeeeirike! His chortle, knee slap and stories
made us laugh. I remember the freshness of the fallen tree branches,
the clear morning air after the rain,
the cleanup we made
into a game.

>Ah lightning, how those cracks and bangs
>rattled my imagination, struck my dreams
>blazed new pathways through
>the forest of my childhood
>ignited my youth

Hot Springs Archeology

Sulfur chalk
coats oak leaves
and dragonfly wings.
Delicate, dry and
perfectly preserved
even under water,
where all is
dissolved
but these salty
petrifaction.

We live with the Geese I

They sail lightly without weight
Without a thought to their
oiled feathers.

They bob,
fat black and white corks
heads pivot on a band
around their graceful necks.

They wait for final
configurations
that will send them soaring
honking madly,

Until they return
Until the pale ice breaks,
and the sweet smell
of wild black soil

wakes us up,
after winter's
heavy snows.

We live with the Geese II

The geese fly over the house
in large gaggles with
wild cackles.

Wind carries their voices
in rounds and fleets
above the lake.

Deciduous trees ring
the lake and the dying year
with this echo.

First Winter Frost

I have to learn to love winter again,
returning to this climate after years away.
I have to learn to relax into it,
in moments when I see
with new eyes

the frost tatting on the edge of leaves,
secret white messages written to me
on the windows in the morning.
The wild arrow of geese over head that call out
pointing the way to warmer climates.

No one really knows what these signs mean,
but they add up, together they tell us,
that soon the snow will sleep the earth to spring,
good parents, winter and summer,
ever present, constant,
tucking us in at night.

But something changes once again and forever,
the way a gentle touch softens a cold night,
at the edge of the lake
the first day of frost.

Winter Migration

Late afternoon
 long strings of geese
        stitch and roll
along the underbelly of clouds.

They sound a call,
       she answers them
and leaves with the geese
       in the night.

They made a proper wake
       to herald her arrival.

Sun Down

Tails flip and
necks stretch,
wings beat
along the water
propelling their flight.

Black cutouts
cruise along the surface
then rise and float
in streams
of honey-orange.

They ripple the air
and alter thunderheads
which skirt the pond
and pass the flock
floating in pools of fire
on the road to nightfall.

Solstice

Clear winter night,
sky and fir tree
ablaze with stars!

December 25

I take a tuck
in the night sky
and wrap stars
around my tree.

Cannea and Calla

Cannea lilies flame
red trumpets above wide green hands
open to catch the dew and available sun.

Among the calla lilies gentle spirals
open slowly, become a partial fan,
a coy invitation, deep opaque goblets
where bees are lost in soft tunnels.

What a blissful way to go - drunk
with sweetness surrendered to the nectar
they lay on their back and buzz to a wobbly stand
covered with pollen - yellow boots and chaps,

they must see a thousand blue sky lids above
in their multiple eyes. Seduced
by the sweet scents they mistake for a mate
they become drunken inmates falling
over and over within the blossom well.

Looking Up through Trees

Crab apple blossoms
open five white petal arms
to happy humming and buzzing.
Intertwined with pine,
embrace of fir spirals
out in needle bursts.

High above them
yellow eucalyptus blossoms,
explode as stars
delight in place
to hold the racket
of countless honey suckers.

Honey bees and bumblebees
legs heavy with pollen
burrow deep
and drunken into
the bodies of flowers
to extract the golden dew.

My back rests
on the soft green Earth
my beehive heart full
of their resonant chorus,
and the endless
turquoise blue.

Morning Ritual Walk

Gold nuggets once
littered this roadside stream.
Now fools gold, pyrite
and mica glisten.

Miners lettuce, blue-eyed grass and yellow violets
are the precious gems now,
were then,
but for feverish miners.

Light through ferns, redwood and oak
dark trunks before me
lighter ones behind
the mist rises from a cool forest.

I ignore
houses,
propane tanks painted green
and barbed wide.

On the looping road
A child's tiny hand waves
all five fingers extending
says a cheery Hi!
I am relieved
she's not a dog
Too many owners with their dogs
in this neighborhood.

Her mother in her jogging suit
and I in sweats exchange good mornings
I wave at her daughter in her wheeled stroller
as they push past.

Neither of them can see
the dog I walk with today.
This fear dog,
a terror of living my wild life

comes with this thought:
'You'd better make friend
with the dogs,
especially in this neighborhood.'
Off the road,
Poison Oak dogs guards the entrance
to the deepest woods.
Crow caws and mountain sorrel greet me.

Moss and decayed leaves, give off a musty
scent in the wild woods, makes the trail spongy.
It has been like this
for thousands of years, why should we change it?

A helicopter slaps the air—I look up then down to
a deep stream slicing through the forest
meandering snake-like down and down—
a single vibrant moss covered log

allows the only crossing.
At the bottom
the ringing of the falls
is the only sound.

I sit on the log for a moment
alone with
my restless
dogs.

On the Altar of Trillium

on the side of the road
where roots tangle and
moss makes a mantle
this is where you grow.

Your three leaves three sepals and
three white petals fade to purple,
cocked adjacent to the collar
of green.

Each petal curls to the right
leaves open to the left slightly
and begins a spiral
out and out

tangling among my own spirals
you a fallen star
caught by
three whirling arms

and I turn and turn
and how the wheels
have turned.

You open me
in the morning
now as you did then
to the surprise of spring.

Then my beloved was outside
myself, he showed me the first
glimpse of your glory.

But he was another lover
flaming out
and I the phoenix once again
have the beloved inside now

and even as you come and go,
here you are again,
would never leave
can never leave,
your bright face
radiant in being you
and perhaps this is what I love,
each of us,
has this bright illusive face.

I have turned away,
but this morning I see you,
this morning, Trillium,
I see my own bright face
in you.

May Haiku

Tight fisted lilacs
our sun soaked trellis bursts
fragrant with blossoms.

Stellar Bird

You pick out bugs
from the bottle brush bark.

Black bead eye,
you sharpen you rapier on the limb,

flip up to another branch,

stand stock still on ink-dipped
feet that glisten radiant.

You preen and oil blue-black fans
step from a carbon pool

Mime of the manzanita.

Sunflowers like Stars

Fog blankets sunflowers and corn rows
in the deep valley below. Sun streaks break
through to yellow petals sparkling like stars.

From the west, Thunder Beings begin ceremony
and slowly reach the shore
as the last flares of sun turn violet.

I stand in my center
on the mountaintop on fire
pen dancing.

Naná - Fresh Water Spring

Naná bubbles her way
through filtering
crevasses
swirls dead leaves,
fallen branches.

Her flow is fresh
pouring into streams
down rivers
over waterfalls
pounds
decomposing leaves.

Naná cleanses all bodies
moves through organs and tissues
is peed out
trickles over rocks to streams
falls underground, through
a filter of roots, earth, rocks,

Bubbles up
from fecund earth
Naná is new again
happy to be happy
pushing foam
into circles that
circle slowly
into this poem.

Chili Pepper Love

Lights of green, red, yellow
on strings of white
a strand of chili pepper
lights surround the Virgin de Guadalupe
Her floral aura a bower of roses
standing on a black moon
an angel cherub lifting it up
she holds her sacred heart.

Next to her
a bouquet of chili pepper lights
in red and green glow
above the door.
The full length of my body
your spirit is here with me
yet I have not heard from you
whether these lights I see before me
are wrapping your heart too.

There are answers
gold, red, blue,
yellow, pink, green
the phone rings!

Pacific Rim

You don't see them come or go
        but they gather on the beach
to pour their hearts into the ocean
        to be with their families for an afternoon
to watch waves roll in
        one after the other.

We came to the sea
        after our personal storm had passed
to walk and rest,
        to fall into silence,
people watch,
        sail boat dream,   sleep.

We felt what was undone,
and let it go
        at the edge of the water.

I gave strands of my hair as an offering,
you sang to the ocean mother
        sounded like a whale.

I was already at the bottom,
recognizing my essence
        in the deep underwater spring.

Then we sat again
like children, like the others,
        in the sand
with our feet dug in, our hands
        drawing full circles, waves

humming an old Indian chant
for the release to the sea
        of what we could not utter
to each other,
        for what we had already
               let go.

Rain, Rain

Rain in barrels
sweat incantations
swells all dryness and spills over
on grass, mud, and a stream of
incoherence on the deck washing clean
etched prints of dog, a 3-toed bird
with a fourth for balance,
the fox's cleaver tail brush away tracks,
so no one can follow him home.

On the roof, the rain taps it's Morris-code,
nervous, nervous knuckle rap
waiting for the phone to ring,
calling anyway, once more anyway,
I want so much to erase the tape
machine with the message I just left
and rain does that
over and over,
if we only had rain phone machines,
as it falls off the roof
over everything
we would only be drawn
into the sound
patting gently,
each moment,
now, drip,
now, drip,
now.

The New Road

It's garbage day, and I am
walking down a new road
on an unfamiliar path.

People are tossing out everything:
spoons and hats, T.V.'s and
tape recorders.

As I pass cans piled high,
I am reminded of the garage sale
we had a few weeks ago,

remains of our marriage
sold after our
years together.

We threw out
the trunk from my ancestor's journey
from Norway to Chicago,

sheets, the shelves for our books
and duplicates of family pictures,
your winter shirts.

We've left it all behind—
you have retired to your tropical island,
and I to my muse, to my

work—right here
on the San Francisco Bay. This is
my home before you and now after.

Then, I pick up a new trail
like drops of blood,
I follow

rose petals laid out precisely
down the sidewalk
one, then the next forming a line.

Each fresh petal perfect, without a bruise,
vibrating deep red on the cold cement,

open,
cupping
the breeze makes them quiver.

The line of red drops stops under an apricot tree.
Fruit hangs ripe, some fallen.

Risk

Like a perfect gentleman he asks, *May I sit with you?*
I am transported to 1892, an English garden party.
Of course, Michael, please have a seat.
In here, his formal manners are refreshing.
I am formal in return.

I look around at the sea of heads.
two of us are women teachers, one woman supervisor,
and four scared young girls in the panel discussion
in a room with 200 men just like their dads in jail.

The Program begins.
A white haired man in a ponytail clear his throat,
plays with the microphone, finds the switch,
turns it on, it squeals. He fumbles his way through.

*Hi, I'm Jack; I'm a former heroine addict, inmate,
and a father of two boys.* The men break into applause.
Got any one man shouts.
Michael looks at me, smiles a nervous grin.
The largest AA meeting in history, he whispers.

I notice he's trimmed his beard; his features are refined,
so handsome, the way he sits down gently, responds to me,
we are suddenly on our first date. I review what
I know of him, he is a blue blood from the East Coast,
he is brilliant, Harvard I think, he loves art, literature,
and he's an alcoholic, his 4th DUI got him in here.

Our program tonight includes a film,
then a panel discussion of these fine young women and men
who have come to share their stories with you,
of what it's like growing up with an incarcerated parent.

*I'll start with mine.
I've been in jail and prison
and missed my first son's childhood.*

I lean over to Michael and whisper,
When do you get out?
July 26th, a little over a month, if all goes well.
Do you have a plan for leaving?
His eyes gloss over, *Not really.*

I've got your certificate for modification,
come by after class with your sheet, I'll sign it for you.
I am his counselor after all
teach substance abuse recovery in county jail.
He was my star pupil. This is his second certificate.

The movie begins. The lights go out.
A wave of caring comes from Michael,
like his namesake the archangel, I am wrapped in
a current of warmth.

I feel his invisible wing touch my blushing cheek.
I am glad it is dark, no one can see my red face.
If we were alone at the movies
his arm would be around me, and we would snuggle in.

My arms keep tightly crossed. He is my student after all.
I focus on the film. Cannot look at him, but instead risk enough
to return the wave, reach my invisible hand out
to touch his bearded face. My spirit kisses him gently,
invisibly on the cheek. If only he weren't in jail ...

After the movie the young people tell
what it was like to place a tiny hand to thick plate glass,
not be able to hug their Dads.
You can hear a pin drop.

Michael leans close and whispers. *I'm glad I never had kids.*
I think of my husband and our lost daughter,
how I wish she'd lived.
The fathers around us are restless. The lights finally come on.
The panel is taking questions. One prisoner asks,
What is your relationship with your Dad now?

One young boy gets up, *My Dad is in prison*
my Mom is in jail. I am out of the Hall on
community service. I never see him but he writes sometimes.
Does that answer your question?

One girl rises, *I am still angry at him.*
Another girl stands and giggles through her talk.
I don't know him. She blurts out.
Another child rises, *He's clean now.*
He tries, but I keep my distance.

Jack grabs the mic, *That's all the time we have*
let's give these kids
a round of applause for having the guts
to stand up here and share with you.

The men burst into shouts and whistles and
clap their approval. *Those kids have so much courage.*
Michael says as he shakes his head. *I remember what it was like*
when I was in college, when I was a T.A.,
how scared I was in front of people.

The men in the room seem to stand
all at once. Suddenly I am in a crush of male bodies.
I sense Michael, the gentleman, the Archangel, at my back
keeping the others at bay. We are in the English garden again.
He is escorting me to my carriage.

We're out of the cafeteria, in the hall.
I'll see you after class. I'd come but
I need a break.

One man blurts out, *Hey, Einstein, you gonna help me tonight?*
Michael nods. Bringing us back into focus,
counselor, student, inmate, teacher, I reply
I'm here if I can help, Michael.
His smile says thanks
his eyes are filled with resignation.
My chest tightens with
      that look in his eye.

Desert Moon

        Amber
          moon
           coyote
            on ridge
          sends
        a howl
      echo
        into its
     golden
cup.

Music

Rain
drips
a symphony

No other
maestro
necessary.

Sanctuary

Surrounded by red clay roofs
four courtyard walls stand
with arches opening the
white silence.

Trees rise and vines cling
bursts of lilies and birds of paradise
begin the arches
where paths meander
from one side
to the other.

Around
a fountain
sprinkling
from central spigot
the gentle lines
of falling water
complimenting the portals
on all sides.

A single bench under
a tree covered in
flowers waits,
a sanctuary for
a troubled soul.

Peace lives in the garden
is cultivated here
like spongy grass under foot
soft curves of violets and
orange Day-Lilies
in fireworks
rim the edges.

And they say that
all the fire you bring
here can be released
to the green
and purple iris.

Wake-Robin
Trillium Ovatum

In the Spring, during the time of Trillium,
white petals
open only to filtered light
wet earth from the first rains
fills them
six yellow stamens,
three-lobed pistil
tie each blossom into
three green open hands.

As these woodland flowers age,
pale pink
brushes the white slowly
on the edges at first.

As more flowers bloom,
bees pollinate
sucking their sweetness,
so they become
more than they were
in their bulbous heart.

As they fade,
dark magenta floods
their faces, edges curl.
Their color signals
the grandmother's
blood held inside

Yet
they still
sing brightly
among the virgins.

More beautiful
as they age,
they are a sign
to me,
of how
to live
an elegant
and
continuous
flowering.

Moon Mirrors

"The fire and the water...accidental, done with mirrors."
Rumi, Book five, v 420-455 from "The Question" in Open Secret
Translation by John Moyne and Coleman Barks.

We all begin in the dark.
Tonight is a warm
womb world.

At 3 a.m. this
black wolf night is
cool and quiet inside too.

Moon light pours in its
relentless platinum light, and
casts the darkest shadows I know.

The hum of the Earth
opens a fire, then
a bubbling spring
inside this moment.

Stillness seems to groan
silence is celebrating itself,
Inside I fall more deeply into
this crack of stillness.

The void has
a floor, the floor is invisible
the ceiling is what we walk on

Darkness is open
changing places with the moon
in an endless tango.

Fog in the Morning

So thick, I can pretend
that the dogs barking
their hollow echoes are wolves,
that the woods on either side
of the road are deep and populated with
ferns and deer.

The houses are invisible and
I am walking within a deep tone
hum of the earth,
through
redwood
and oak
alone and aligned
to all that lives.

I am woven
from milk weed and milky way
a single star
shooting across the sun warmed sky
almost invisible above the land clouds
yet felt with the fingers of fog
opening
lifting, letting go.

Thick vapor is
wrapped tightly
around everything
just after dawn.

THE EMERALD SELF

Stained Glass Sun

Before we invented medicine
the only thing that lay between
the people and death was light.
Families lay their sick ones
beneath the colored windows of cathedrals.

They knew better than we
that first there is the pierced heart,
then the rearranging of light rays
by that unseen hand
as the sun moves across the glass.

This initiation surrenders
every fragment of who
you thought you were
taking long draws
on straws of light
until you revive or move on
under the stained glass sun.

The Emerald Self

There, in this heart-field of
deep grass
the missing gem
that was
lost

to be found only by
star gazing
or sitting
by the frog pond

Joy!

Redwood Wedding

A rock shaped like a heart
inside a tree?

I curl into it
and sit in the deep drone
it makes, regarding its curves
and resident spiders.
I am at home here.

Others come blowing by
but do not change
the music inside the tree.

A child cries in the distance.
Flute notes drift up from the valley.
Rusty bark catches the light.

There is a wedding going on inside.

Owl Medicine

Owl, screeching through the forest,
stops me in my tracks.
It flies past so fast
it could not see me.

Then as if it heard my thoughts it turns,
looks straight at me, it's eyes are blue,
like mine. She stares at me with my eyes,

Inside now
she shows me these deep pools of seeing all,
inside she hears because it is in me.
Wings so light they barely weight a thing.

Her beak so sharp
you would not feel
the cut.

she is saying,
I am death, stealth,
predator, prey

I am in you.
Befriend me,

Lift with my wings,
fly with me now

from flight,
you will sing
your calling.

Carrion Flower

Certain rare birds
     can regrow wings and learn to fly again.— Raggedy Andy

I keep her in a metal cage,
outside my heart garden,
wings clipped, exiled—too dangerous to be let out—
I could keep an eye on her here,
This way, she won't hurt anyone, I'm sure.
She suffers 1000 tortures from other lives
I can't stand her screams
so I bring her a single rare flower,
a Carrion Flower, black tongue licking out
of a purple ruffled wing,
it smells like its name.
She smiles her caged up grin
and I ask if she is able to hear me,
her head bobs in all directions,
I can't tell if the answer is yes or no
I love you the way you are,
and you are in here for a good reason!
The last words roll into the sewer
as lost coins. The real truth?
I am afraid of her.
Given half a chance she would kill me—
first for ignoring her—then for locking her up.
So on the next visit,
I bring her more flowers with different scents
all in pots so they are living beings
first daisies, then tulips then a whole field of daffodils.
She looks through the bars at me and laughs
then organizes herself into a lotus position
on the cold floor, tears damming under her eyes.
After a while, in a veil of golden smoke
she sprouts her new wings and
disappears, and somehow
takes the flowers with her!

I put the skeleton key into the lock
and opened the empty cage.
She leaves me a note,
I didn't know she could write,
Your turn honey,
now it's your turn to
surrender. Ha, ha!

Star Baby

She came through
the Milky way
her skin galaxies
her wild eyes fathomless
black holes, brown stars
new sparks fly with
each twinkle

Star baby innocent essence
who made her this way
new and ancient
untamed
divine
night?

White Turtle Woman, the Earning of My Name

Maybe there are turtles, Maybe grief is swimming by...
                                                    Julia Alter

In Puerto Rico, women never travel alone,
but on the Island of Culebra
I had to hike to the open sea
where thunderstorms devour green islands,
black and white and blue and green.

Up a mythic trail, I step around two snakes
it is the name of the island after all.
Ascending from a gentle inland
shore to the other side, stormy waves are crashing in.
I see the storms swallowing our names,
Mari luna del Sol, White Turtle Woman,

Sea and Moon of the Sun, piercing storms
I see your name in this hungry rage
in the sun spots on blue water.
I see my dive to the depths of the sea
A deserted coral beach greets me.

I don't have to walk through fear, but as I do
Under the surface the water is calm,
I see huge racks of stag horn coral,
Brain coral the size of Volkswagen bugs,
graceful hands of fans wave on.

I don't have to swim through her loss, but as I do,
the sun breaks open new worlds to me
invisible plankton and jellies pass by
a black and white turtle swims out and about
pipe fish, parrot fish, and clown fish dive.

How odd, my life returns after she is gone,
salt water swims in coral pools,
she gives tender turns of fishes' fins,
and offers a clown turtle that sees me now
she gives black fish with blue-eyed tails.

My child died so I could live
her spirit is a woman now,
black and white turtle swims with me,
paints, becomes and reveals more of me,
and I am no longer an empty shell.

White Turtle Woman dives at the edge of the sea
Rises like lightening to the starry sky
and she has opened both doors for her mom.

Mari travels along with me.
She swims through joy in this vacant love,
Sea and moon of the sun remains
Mari Luna del Sol is here and not.
Black and white and blue and green,

Storms pass through other lands now.
My heart aches for those in that stormy path.
How could we forget to give earth to her name?
And the sun shines after my storm has gone.
Mari Luna missed her earth and became a star
Sin la tierra, el mar, la luna y el sol hacen una estrella.

This moon has faded in our daylight love,
I empty my shell in this moonlit pool.
El mar y el sol y la tierra quedan.
The sea and sun and earth remain.

The Master and The Miser

The master says, The more you give away the more you have.
The miser says, The more I keep the more I have.
The master says, You have done so well protecting your money
and look you have barely had enough.
The miser says, Thank you, I made sure we had just enough.
The master says, Look how the money flows into our coffers
and flows out to the greater world.
The miser says, How did you do that?
The master replies, Generosity is the heart of God.

The miser says, I don't know how to do it, I am not enough.
The master says, Who taught you that? That is a lie. You are enough.
The miser says, It was told me when I was just a child,
then that lifetime I spent in the cave eating rats,
all was lost, and then I turned it around again
with my savings and scrimping and eating garbage.
The master says, That was not you,
but the large hand of grace that helped you up again,
after you refused to surrender.
The child was afraid of the power and beauty given,
the soul does not know about 'not enough',
please don't speak it so life can live!

Then the miser says, Master can you teach me to open my hand?
The master says, It depends on you own master within.
Go ahead, try it; open your heart now.
And the miser opens first his fist over his heart
his heart hurts from the contractions and paralysis relaxing
Then it began fluttering like a spring, and he lay spread open
pouring out tears
weeping
grinning
grateful.

Red Baby Blues

I'm bonding with Red Baby, Daddy
the one who has no voice.
I'm bonding with the red one, daddy
so the child will have a choice.

I'm bonding with Red Baby, Baby
the one inside of me
bonding with this bloody Baby, yeah!
the one that's not so pretty

She's the one who paints the garden, Ma
thirty-three shades of gray
then the weeds change color, daddy, all
to her great gray dismay

I've got this child home with me today.
She loves to make a fuss,
I'm bonding with feisty baby, yeah!
Crying only soothes Baby

I'm bonding with Red Baby, Mama
its not a pretty sight
first she throws the orange paint, Daddy-o
she loves to pick a fight.

Yesterday I cleaned up Baby, Ma
a tragic night before,
then I held my breath and temper, Dad
while she mopped up the floor

I'm bonding with Red baby, Daddy
The one, oh yeah the one
I haven't heard before.

Past Life Lie – 1753 Reclaimed 2005

I follow a black root deep inside,
so deep no one saw it before
winding between rocks
tendrils of grief
going down into forgotten soil
into subterranean crevices
so deep it grows underwater
an underground ocean
it grows other roots inside my past
the same cave
going down,
down
through the heart of the Mother.

The story is the same one
from all our pasts;
someone doesn't like
who we are;
First we other,
then invent
then eliminate.

'You're too powerful,
too good, too bad,
too much, they act against us,
or we against them, they make up
stories about us.
Some maybe true, others console
their fears with the lie of our too small selves.
Another witch hunt
played out over and over.
The stake is waiting, we burn.

They become afraid of what they could
become, what we each are.
Our cycles are tied onto the mill wheel slaves,
embarrassed for our invisible sins.
Lie machinery grinding
us into dust.

The real story is how fear
keeps us in our place, the place
someone else makes for us.
"What makes you think your so good!"
Crabs of culture pulling us back
into that same stinking bucket.

But they forgot, we forgot
That our place is with the stars
singing, dancing wild shooting stars
or in the arms of the sea
rocking on her broad breast
hauling up the anchor on the last tendrils
of that old root, are fusing our shattered light,
feel it, love streams unfettered
in this next initiation.

First pour over our bowed heads
beer, milk, finally the flowing honey,
our hair alive with bees outside our silent brains.
Our hair dripping with love
the sweetness of what is here all
the time bringing the All
around us, through us, no 'I' only
flowers falling through into open palms
where a resonant hum
cracks open
a new chorus.

Sprout

My hand is not a hand
      but a single wing
a shadow, shroud,
      my palm
patting seeds in place.

Who knows if it will sprout
      or die
blossom or disintegrate
Perhaps the best this seed can do
      is to be food for a hungry jay
who may find it first
      and ignite its desire
for more
      pecking
mating
  scratching
flight.

Sundance

We flock like inland Pelicans
black and white birds of a feather
to dance together.
Choke-cherry branches tied horizontally
as arms stretched out, make the tree
a relative, a human being,
one people-tree offered willingly
for life to continue.

Slowly we dance and blend
white husbands and red mothers
children golden brown,
black-haired and blonde.

We cry together
share our losses
pray in the sweat lodge,
suffer the same.

Empty chairs of the recent dead
line the arms of the arbor
surrounding the dance grounds
we come to freeze, heal,
die, pray and release
who we thought we were.

No more white or red,
yellow or black, just
one flock circling the tree
all natives of Turtle Island.

Extinction of the Phoenix

Did you know that before the Peacock the Phoenix came first?
Those wise peacock eyes glowing green and purple
like a royal cape of jewels,
their grace and strut was
not just deemed,
no,
their shimmering was earned,

disaster after disaster, eye after eye,
before Phoenix went extinct, before
the designer said,
Enough!

It was then the fiery bird declared, Wait!
Consumed in flames again only to be
reborn of its blackened egg and
climb its perch to shake off
the burning lessons, it
surrendered
once again
and again
until it could declare,
Yes!

Its countenance and wisdom expanded,
in a backwards sort of way,
just to be sure to get
Peacock

right.

Honey Strands

It is time to wash
and braid my hair,
to sit alone
and watch the bees,
to hive within myself
taste honey.

Now is the time for weaving,
of gathering sweetness
humming golden fiber
into my being.

It is time to compose
my internal fabric.
To begin my tapestry
from what has fallen
to the floor.

What I know about Mariluna

My daughter is nine feet tall,
her hair, a shoal of stars.
She teaches me to love myself
despite her loss.

Her hands are open galaxies
ready for me to ask anything
She loves everyone abundantly.

She lives with my Mother, Grandmother,
Grandpa too
She teaches from what she knows
bringing in radiance

I listen to their voices in soft whispers
feel their hands touch mine on the key boards
yes we are here, yes we are here for you
they come to my husband too.

It is confusing they are here in spirit
and not in a body
daily I grieve and celebrate
Walk between this world and that one
they are worlds apart
yet immediate to the other.

We roam the Earth,
look in the microwave
talk on the internet,
what are we really looking for
when it is right here
in this cage of ribs,
this beating pulse,
a sigh.

What Promises Have You Made?

In another life, I was a nun
wandering in and out of hollow halls,
praying to whomever could hear me.

We had a place to live
and food to eat
and made ourselves servants of the poor.

There was no Salvation Army
no St. Vincent de Paul.

But today, I must release
that old vow of poverty,
it has kept me in survival too long

Open the convent door
to my freedom
let these braids be unraveled

Walk in that sultry way
almost forgotten
along any road you choose

Among the leopards and the jaguars
feel your wild animal writhe and curl
stretch in the blaze of sun.

Hum of the Earth

When we finally know
our truest self
will we be able to describe,

How light and dark are from
the same source,
cascade into us
unceasingly?

How the Earth supports us
relentlessly
all fire and stone
Could we hear her hum?

Would we sit in dumb awe
of this mountain or
in rapt attention as
fish silver through streams.

Could we describe
the burst of our own light
when we really let go.

Could we take flight
become the air
with the gliding
heron
lifting us
with her wings?

Immersion

It's a Poindexter feeling
round-glasses-hide-in-the-chem-lab feeling
an I-don't-want-to-go-out-of-the-house feeling
don't-touch-me-I'm-not-your-friend feeling

It's a this-world-is-too-hard feeling
How-can-I-make-it feeling
It's a no-money-and-no-way-to-get-there
feeling

It's a deep-debt-drowning feeling
How-can-I-possibly-do-it feeling?

The drums say,
go in, find your feet
They are on the Earth

I dance the feelings out
stomp them out
dance hard
ask for help.

Rest now,
feel the wave
that-it's-over feeling
Andromeda is waving
her arms
in relief.

The Muse Finds Me
inspired by Joseph McNeilly

Where are you?

I am here
have not gone anywhere,
I am the waiting cat

Here on the ledge,
on your roof
watching your busy life.

Where are you now?

Look behind the waterfall
in the spring that gushes
from deep in the earth.

Follow me down now
That damp chilly cave
is me, the source of all waters

Where blind fish swim
where rocks are
walls, ceiling, floor

This cave is eternal and hidden
a moist and mossy floor where light
opens through the roof.

Where there is no light
this   is
where I dwell

You hear only
a slight
gurgling spring

This alone
is
who you are

Reach for me now,
feel the cool damp
places in yourself

Hear nothing
but your rhythmic
heart pounding.

Sparrow

My voice makes you more nervous, little bird shudders and flutters around a windows.

My nest, my mate, chicks, I hear them, see them, cannot fly there, cannot fly there

No inside nor outside to this bird. Just light, in light you are free to fly everywhere. Not here. Oh not here.

Thin hard rock wall, I see them, cannot fly there, this clear wall will not let me through, not let me through, I cannot fly through it, cannot crawl through it, yet light there is light.

Poor thing, words do not help at all, you shudders more, and fly at the kitchen window as I approach.

Who is it, who is it, this call booming oh, I die here, who is it, who is, fly where she is not, fly away, just move away, more light more hard clear wall, I am caught on this ledge, see trees, cannot fly away.

Heart beating,   pounding,   caught in a cage of fear, looking to be eaten. I wrap your tiny body in a green towel.

Comes again, too loud, closer, I die, spiders, webs, comes with green moss over me, smells no moss, feels no moss, there is no way out, she comes, she comes, buries me. Soft claws around me, green moss cloth, this is it, this is it, her eyes so big, teeth, she shows her teeth, where is my nest, my safe nest. I die.

You see the open door. I relax my hands.

Oh opening, oh door, claws loosen, I wiggle free, wiggle free, open wings, open wings, yes, I fly out, open wall, yes, fly past nest, sing, fly free
  yes!

Neptune's Church

He lights a candle
drawing our attention
from cliff's edge
to altar

Inside a jade plant grows
in a pot of earth
sage smolders in a shell
our two drums ready
a rattle painted with birds
fly across the gourd

our deck of tarot cards
his shell
Neptune gave him
in Puerto Rico

my sacred pipe
the basket
that holds more sage

our good wishes
for each other
prayers for family
into the night
all rest on the table

I light a leaf of sage
to begin.

Traveling Towards Dawn

Worship this forest blue egg moment;
walk over sand dunes near sea tides.

Take this lusty wind and drive
through shark jaws and hyena moon howls.

Those wild dogs will dig all night in hillsides
and make land melt into rivers.

Walk quickly past the pack, slowly escape, steady, ride the scooter
which hurries this tin whistle go cart strangely around the next curve

Now baffle your pursuers, banish your fears to the dig.
Abandon their terror residue,

Unplug from the waves of silicon ingots
with that champion overdose of computer chips.

Slide in wet earth on your way down.
Hold onto the cedar branch, wear your muddy head.

You are almost there so walk steadily to your cottage,
spoon with your lover, sigh,

Drink from the calm inland lake, dawn,
the safety of being new.

Firelight

Someone plays with fire
on the beach
They twirl pots of flame
spinning along dark waves
darkening sky
as flames go out
sand has lost its colors
as cigarette stars try to
poke through ink
then fog   then clear
someone lights up
lights on a mast
sail along a dark
invisible horizon.

Turtle Massage

Before the land existed there was only water...After many failed, Toad dove deep into the water...bringing the Earth up from the depths and placed it on Turtle's back. At once the Earth began to grow larger and larger until it became the whole world..."
Woodlands Indians story of how the Earth came into being

She rocks my shell slowly
ploughs the field
long abandon,
she loosens compacted shoulder soil.

Take a deep breath now...

She digs to let the light in, air,
Water flows down trenches
through clotted loam
in fields ready to plant. Water seeps
through black earth
between hardened rocks, drips through cave cracks
where drops trickle to an underground stream,
flows out to a lost pond.

In the center, a turtle floats,
dives deep underwater,
sinks to the bottom.

Turtle finds no enemies, no threats
Lies between rocks as a rock.
Water stirs far above,

Gentle rocking, rocking my shell.
I slip out for one moment,
leave my shell behind.

This turtle lies pink and naked on the bottom.
I take a breath, float up and up
to find finger spades smoothing earth in place.

Turn over please...
Turtle complies, dissolves
my shoulders
loosen enough to grow
seeds of ease.

Her hands gather hair shafts,
form sheaves and sheaves of golden wheat.
My face loosens with her fingers that
slide, stop release

Rest now...

Turtle sighs, sees
milkweed pods pop open
seeds blow free
over autumn fields.

Masseur

He has the right mix
of firm and flair
slip and
glide,
in total control,
as he rolls down my back
with his elbow.
Muscles kneaded
with his art-touch
and love
that exudes
from his fingertips.

He flips the sheet and
tucks it close to my thigh

as he strokes the quad
to release.
My body
convulses
he says
softly,
never mind,
Your body is
just unwinding.

Outside a waterfall
flows over coy,
and around
bulrushes.

Inside,
all the stress
of the week
follows a leaf
downstream.

Norma's Dream

Flowers moving out

                         from the Mother rose

        only she has

                         purple stripes

    Roses in all stages

                         of opening,

dozens of women

                         of all colors

dressed in white,

                         flowing skirts

  bringing baskets

                         of rose offerings

  for this first tree

                         a rose bush

    full and broad

                         grown into

      the tree of life

               a horn of plenty

            for everyone.

For Those Who Are New to Grief

Wear cotton batting
around your soul.

Tell the story to those
who will hold it like a duckling

then release it safely
in gentle pond waters.

Take walks by rivers
through woods

or on the beach at night
to avoid crowds.

Stay away from loud
or obnoxious people

offering advice or analysis.
Walk away if you can't take it.

Just know, you have been catapulted
into new waters,

into a deeper world,
where ocean tides

continually take you,
sometimes when you least expect it,

and landing with ones who know
becomes your best solace.

Ewa
(pronounced Āwaa)

Emerging from air she dissolves invisible. In Brazil she is called Ewa, mist, fog, who rises from ponds, and wraps around everything. She is embodied in a young girl dancing on the edge of a dock. Mist rises to honor her in broad daylight. Innocent, sad Ewa, waits around the cemeteries for her grandparents to wake up from their deep sleep. She waits for them to take her to the circus. Her lament is engulfing. She swirls around their headstones tenderly.

Up on the ridge on Mt. Tamalpais, bright sun, high cirrus clouds, below layers of Ewa, cotton batting, her mist infiltrates trees, glides around birds, buildings, cars, all colors of skin, gangster or saint, mountain lions hiding in trees, napping squirrels, beer cans, pieces of trash, jays, ravens, advertisements, shoppers, egrets, San Quentin, Great Blues and sandpipers, still dodging waves as they always do in their twittering steps in and out and around the waves as Ewa cries her name; Ew-a-a-a-a

Her cool touch engulfs the grieving, drunks or addicts, spills over farmers, cows, barns, sheep, Ewa lingers. She touches Tule Elk, albino deer, spiders, she shows us their invisible webs, lizards those sneaky surprises that always startle, she touches everyone and everything the same. From the ridge, I blow a small eagle plume off my hand down to her cheek. Ewa, you sad virgin-child, what a cold lovely cotton blanket you bring.

Illusion of Blue

Heron wades
on a wooded river bend.
Sun dapples her back as
feathers ruffle and
impossible long legs
bend backwards.
She pretends
not to notice me
then moves off.
Savoring her wild form,
settling deeper into the grass,
she hears stirs
then lifts those
great arched wings
stretches her beak of a
pterodactyl out

                    crooks her neck   flap after flap
                            further   down   stream.
                                From inside bend of the river
                                    She lands, is surprised again,
                                        this private bird flaps
                                        her   way   away.
                                    Flowing   riverofbird,
                                quite   pond,
                            hidden marsh,
                        she
                    disappears.
                        Her grey
                            only blue
                                in direct sun,
                                    this reflected
                                        flash flies around
                                                    inside.

What We Don't Say

How love has settled its claws
into this chest, belly, root

How in my dream the men crouch in the dark around the fire
whispering their failures to one another - fear dogs in the shadows

How the women play with babies
not yet able to speak another language

How a stream of adolescents just walked past me on the trail
How two young girls walk and talk a private language together

How the boys have no hair on their legs yet
How we have so little time, really

How a firebird flew in to light the fires for the men
While a new tongue is being formed for women

How straight you are, how bent
How straight I am, how bent

How the thrumming never ceases
how your fear is healing, how mine is being seen

Night Thorns

In the dark, thorns of longing
tangle in scarf, shirt

Fingers pricked
torn asunder.

All night, in my dream,
a polar bear robe

surrounds me
held, talking to my teachers.

After, roses fell
in white cream sky.

Fukushima mon amour

This morning its reactor #4
I worry about.
Years after the meltdown,
it's still leaking.
And the Japanese government
maintains everything is
under c-o-n-t-r-o-l.

The news media calls them out
in cautious dribble. Videos on You-Tube
show the Geiger counters going crazy
off Fukushima's coast. Rebel scientists
are testing their own samples of earth, air,
water from that nuclear fire.

Surfing could be dangerous
for your health. Boating and swimming
are a cautionary tale.
What can we eat from the ocean
now?

My neighbor says that
everything on the west coast
is already contaminated
200 miles inland
from Portland to San Diego.
She is keeping her surfing sons
out of the water.

I don't believe everything I hear,
so I will sit in meditation
then have breakfast.
We can decide how to wrap our love
around this pattern of human
self-destruction spilling out.

I start with myself.
Einstein said over and over,
'Everything is energy.'

So in my monthly meditation group
we send a flotilla of light boats and submarines
from our hearts through the waters
neutralize this nuclear waste
reverse the wave of light, dissolve it,

send in a blanket of absorbent flowers
on the backs of paper cranes
to the people of Japan.

Before the Phoenix

Paste the feathers
of one more disaster onto bones
that are shattered, scattered.

Like a beggar who tries to make
sense out of another useless
night, look for scraps
among the debris.

After the shock wears off
through coal cold lumps held
in a fist, the tears come,
so gather up the pieces,
open your hands,
let them tumble out together,
on to the stone altar.

Wait and wait for them to cool.
Sift the burnt offerings,
exhaust them.
Then release the last fistful
of ash.

Death of the Death Wish

Make a whistle from my thigh bone
when I die,
let the eagles hear the laughter
from my bones.

Let this be a surprise to everyone,
how death is a song,
and sorrow makes way for soaring,
well into the evening sun.

Silver Thread

I heard their honking first
a flock of something
rolling beyond

Looking up to pale blue skies
a shimmering string
now two break over
knurled branches of spidery oaks

So far away I cannot count them,
these geese or ducks,
perhaps snow geese with their white wings,
their arrow shapes, two silver ribbons
turn in the sun.

Now a red tail or eagle soars higher
with them or below, I cannot tell
who it is
what it is,
just it's span larger
than two of them.

Perhaps their furious warnings
keeps the talons curled
and not extended
for one of them.

They furl
and twist
one string
sheltering the other.

Suddenly the great bird
takes a different course
I notice a shadow is
pulled out of me,

I remain transfixed
by these shining strings,
their secret display and
I am pure silver inside

when they disappear
as I glance away.

Desert Walk

She is a half moon shard
in a crystal sky
ready to fall away

A mad woman walking
on red desert rocks
craving water

Water sinking
into dry sand
sand melting into glass shards.

She carries a cracked walking stick
on no path familiar
Nor a path well trodden

There is no other trail.

Star Woman

I met you in the dark,
immense
awesome
drum dancing
you took our
daughter's spirit
home.

Now you come to say:
I catch all souls in
my starlit arms
No one is lost
in my shadow veils

Each one has a place
to grow, to live.
No one is left alone
to die.

You say:
Your daughter is
my daughter too.
I open my
star-filled arms.

No one is left to drift
in the Milky Way,
all have stars
of their own found
in the folds
of my silken
robes.

Impression

In the grass
damp with dew
with halos of spider webs,
I am drawn
in and
down belly to
Earth.

I pour out
all those losses
that have shaped me.
The daughter I cannot hold,
mother
as she slipped
out of her body
while the touch of
her feet grew cold,
the loss and loss of loves past,
friends who now
move in different streams,
and the loss of who I was before
I met you.

All sink deep into
loam soft from winter rains
opening
a space for me,
forming an imprint
of my body
in the vibrant grass
and what remains
is a quiet song
ringing
inside this
empty
cage.

Water Windows

Stepping through a window
from a cool stone lodge
down the bright trail to the banks
of the Tuolumne River, where a
blue sky-dome is reflected in ripples
and invisible fish roil clouds,

I make a frame between thumbs and forefingers
around a green grass dot on a sandbar
amongst gray rocks with water
vibrating cerulean blue.

Climbing out on a ledge further and further
bare-footed, bent over to stare into
another window to see if perhaps a fish
or a minnow school will swim by,
I am five again, at home belly to stone on
warm rocks where fish forage, minnows dart,
crawfish skitter sidewise.

As at so many turning points I gaze into water,
it is a return home for me,
I feel that child on Lake Michigan,
the girl in the Smoky Mountains,
a young woman near Lake Superior
navigating slippery rocks
cold snow-melted pools and rivers
ambling around everything.

Inserting my hand this time into river rush
I recognize me in this place
as those rocks
as water in water,
this chirp of chipmonk, sparrow,
clouds as they make a
light-ribbon undulating
through and through.

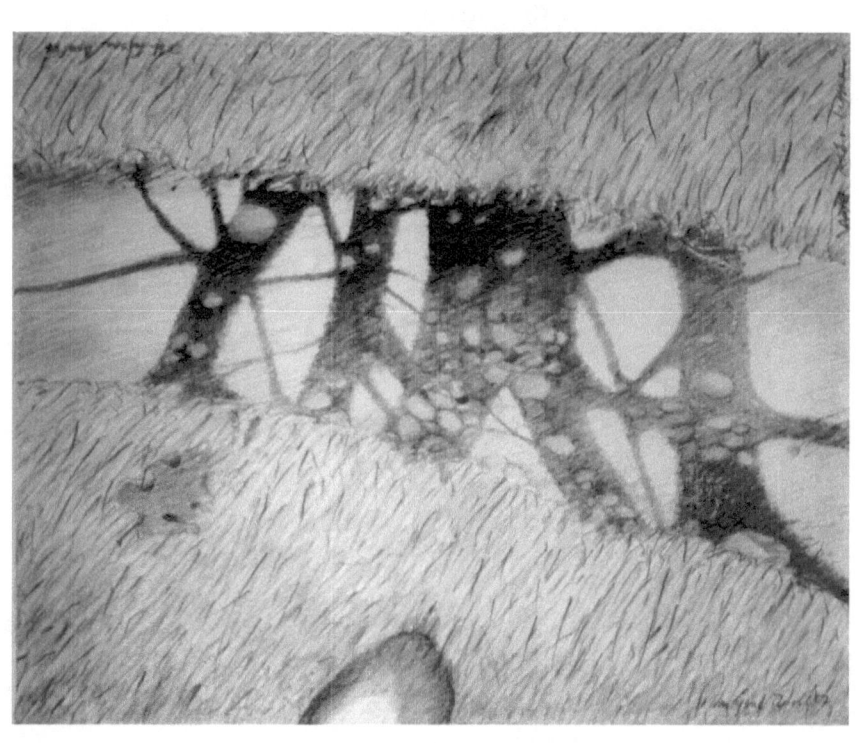

The Writer and the Mother Finally Talk

The author in me lays her pen down again
listens to the mother's sobs
through the thin curtain that separates their rooms.
She rises slowly opens the curtain.

      I would have been a good mother

The author sees the mother 's
suicide note lying
next to her on the bed.

The writer extends her hand,
Come with me, Get Up!

The mother blows her nose,
sits then stands reluctantly,
allows the writer to help her up.

Halfway to the writer's room
the mother wrenches
her hand away.

      Stop. Just stop pulling me
      Stop!

The writer turns,
opens her inky-stained hands
offers a full embrace.

The mother sobs
and collapses again
in her friend's arms.

The two of them sink to the floor
together. In their slide the
spotted curtain is pulled down around them.

The writer touches her cheek
brings out a cloth she used to sop up ink.
Gives it to the mother to dry her tears.

Her face, a striped mask,
she has become the magician
the writer knows and loves.

      I just want to be normal again.

The writer looks at her puzzled
then throws her head back and
laughs.

Tears roll down her cheeks,
with the inky cloth
she makes her own mask,
drying her own tears.

Hysterical now, she gets it.

You never were normal,
whatever that is,
you never fit into convention.

Always the raven
flying its own way
against the wind's currents.

Crow woman, your still-birth
is over! Take up you pen-sword
give birth to bright star poems!

Stop your belly aching
your driving me crazy!

Or keep crying and
drown us both!
Give up the dream
you were given
by your Mother.

A small cottage by the stream,
a black phone
with a manual dial.
That was the 50's honey.
Not now.
The dream of the perfect
life is over.

Let's kill it together
write its epitaph
in its scourge!

The mother grows tired
of the writers talk

    But I wanted a real baby!

I know, I know
Here, come here.

    But do you still love me,
    even if I get teary
    even thought the waves come?

I have cherished every tear
written down every sob
It is how much I love you.

    All this time
    I thought you were ignoring me.

The two finally
embrace long and well,
melt into each other

sit together
inside the other
striped masks, spotted cape
thrumming.

Be Careful What You Say to Yourself

Release the old fear jackets
I'm not good enough
I don't deserve love,

Whoever told you that
in the first place
were liars or fools.

When you smile
the sun bursts out
when you frown

everyone weeps and
tornadoes and hurricanes
start to spin with you.

Don't you see
love,
what you bring
to the other
faces
of love?

Cat Dream

A spotted leopard comes
to lay against my tent

My breath halts
becomes   irregular

I suck in
then
blow out
each breath.

After a long time
this huge cat rises,
stretches its lean body

Makes its long strides
into another tent
set up next to me.

Big enough for a hundred people
two women and a little girl are
preparing a feast

I see them
and try to warn them;

Psst...It's a leopard,
it's wild be careful!

One woman stops her scurrying
and looks over her shoulder;

Yes, so what?
He lives among us

come sister
why not you?

Backyard Vision Quest

Imagine, meditating in the hammock late one night.
Suddenly the doors to another world blow open.
All the guests come in.

We've been waiting, is it time now?

I thought I was hosting a backyard party,
but what enters to form the gathering are
my lost orphans.

'Come in, I say, I didn't know
there were any of you left
to return home. '

Entering the garden with
caution, the children are not sure
if they will be seen or heard

Soon we become a choir of
harmonizing wolves
baying with the full moon.

Moon comes down to us
opens her wide veils
and takes us to her belly.

She laughs and
weeps with us until we
are all exhausted.

Sun peeks his head in,
says,
'Darling, the parties over.'

Moon, slips back
through her veils,
into the heavens. I lie

grinning like a sleeping child,
presents open
under a tree of lights.

Cocoon

If ever you think
caterpillars
have it easy
think again.

First they eat and eat
and eat for fat
will keep them warm
through long winter months.

They spin spider lace
around a milkweed branch and
their plump green form,
they spin for days.

Worst of all, once enclosed
they cook and cook and cook
for weeks in that golden shell
of everything they are.

So total a surrender
there is nothing
as easy as this
nor as impossible.

Caterpillars are then required to melt,
into the unknown of
What shall I become?

Some become a light flash and disappear.
Others surrender into the melting
of their pieces
in the heat of presence—their body
and new wings compose.

When it is time,
they are not done,
they cannot fly right away,
They have to eat their way out.

A Monarch crawls
slowly, slowly, slowly
out of its cocoon, to
flip and stretch moist wings.

In agony
new bones
shake, expand
spread

orange, black, red
to dry
on the same branch
twice as big as their cocoon

until they become art
until they lift as a traveling
cathedral
window.

Beloved

I wander with you
everywhere
we never cease
from making love

Suddenly you're here
inside now outside
in every tree and shrub
in the rain of plum blossoms

Beloved, you are so close
I whisper and it is you I here
singing my true name.

Night Mind

The night sky is my mind
and all the stars are out
there is no limit above,
soft Earth inviting me to play.

There is no limit above
all the stars are out
the night sky is my mind
Earth is soft and inviting

Playing on the Earth
my heart is full of stars
no where else to go
here, full of wonder.

No where else to go
my heart is full of stars
playing on the Earth
here, full of wonder.

Full of wonder I play
a child full of heart
no where else to go
all the stars are out.

Healing Art

I am gushing with
palm trees,
fireworks,
the rotating roots
of an Olive tree,

Cactus hands open,
Yucca spines
layers of vines

are free from a snip
of my scissors.

Odd how nature
loves repetition

Cactus merges with tropical roots
Yuccas spray open
like the Fourth of July.

Crab tracks lead to its hole
on Flaminco Beach some where
on a Puerto Rican Isle.

These images remind me that
everything goes in
before reentering the world.

In the next hour
of making this collage
a client comes to my door
full of bursting open
trying to go out,
when I see her crabby tracks
leading her in instead.

Just breathe into your heart,
tell me what is there.

She is suddenly in the hospital room
with her dying mother.

No one could utter
'I don't want you to die.'

Thirty years of barricaded tears
break open.
I ask her to bring
all the shattered bits of self home.

In come fragments
of suspended grief
floating in her auric field.

They rush in and merge
with her inner family,
her renewal
a true homecoming.

Now she can burst
like the fireworks scattering
the remaining black bits
turning to confetti.

She is drying
her tear storm
under a clacking
palm tree.

It appears to be
the same one
in my collage.

Ode to Orishas

Blood pulses locked in rivers
breath in it's silent rhythm
yours or mine
moves in and out, this force is
Ogum as

Acids churn our food into nutrients.
blood river rush or muscles that fire,
these Xangô bones stand upon themselves.

Who is living me now?

Orishas are the river of life in me,
is the river of Oxum feeding you

Green and living Earth,
laughter of
Oxumaré on her way over
the rocks of
Xangô.

He is the one
who changes everything
strikes justice and lightening
brings into form,
calls it like it is, while
Grandma Naná
hears your gentle sobs.

Oxossi the hunter
and protector
runs through the forest
to find his lover Jurema.

She falls through the trees
lights this path
then that one.

He loves her and chases her
but never catches her.

She lights over Obá, the mud,
first wife of
Xangô, then Oxum,
whose bubbling
makes him laugh.

And Iansa, the wind
who wears away stone
slowly persistently
nags away at Xangô,

Those winds of deserts
change over Tempo,
who looks
at the cowries dropped in sand
taken from Iemanjá.

A fox runs across
circles and sage
Ifa reads your inquiries,
holds the light of Oxala
in her arms.

Are they what lives us,
a circle around
our central flame?
What is Earth in us?

Who is nearest now,
this loving one
standing beside me
singing
my true
name?

Red-tail Lesson

A Red-tail hawk hovers above me
in the stiff wind.

Head takes a slight turn and
it dives to the right.

Head to the left and it moves
in line with the steady
invisible current.

Wings make two sails,
perfect for the hover.

There is no search for food
no survival at stake,

This bird is having fun,
only practicing what it loves

—to speak to the wind by surfing it—

immersing itself
in that for which it was made.

Perhaps it is the bird's yoga, wings open
a Red-tail salute to the sun.

Perhaps it is praying to wind
as she caresses those huge wings.

Perhaps this moment is why it mates,
raises its young, searches for fish.
Grace.

A single moment in perfect trust,
being splendid,
excellent,

one.

Sitting in the Mediation Hall

Thrumming inside, I wait and listen
Creator speaks,

Beloved, hear the many names of mine

John, Mary, Sylvia

Wait I say.
Those aren't names of yours.

Oh, you like, Krishna, Buddha, Jesus?

That's better I say.

Beloved, if you do not know
John, Mary and Sylvia
Roger, Fred and Wendy,
as this one

how can

you know

me at all?

Affinity Sign

In the dark of a graying day

we sit within circles of our two tribes

one full of those who want to bring more light
to this world

another full of those who want to make more art
for this world

they are the same circle
in different cities

an infinity sign

we are at the intersection

standing shoulder to shoulder

as we face each other

hands interlocked.

Wolf Medicine

You lay in the snow,
an ink spill,
yet occasionally
twitch, with your
yellow-eyed stare.

Your ears are black void cones
hearing every mouse nibble
snow flake fall.
You hear trees creek
and my ragged breath.

Your fur is dark as a Raven's wing
so thick cold snow does not penetrate
the brush of your tail
sweeps the snow once where you lie
flurries dust lace around your patient face
your fangs hide
within your closed jaws.

Playing or hunting I cannot tell
our eyes lock
there is no way out
you are my medicine
we make our pact.

Jasmine Pearl

Enter the tea house where
burls of maple slabs have been
made into tables, the tops carved and polished.
Hot water is
poured over the Buddha by the server,
over the cup to warm it,
as swirls down a hidden drain
match maple shimmer.
The steaming cup in my hand
is full of fragrance.

As I sip the tea, inhale the scent,
I see in my cup
a woman from a small Chinese village
whose job it is to
lay out flower petals over leaves
to infuse them over and over.
She then rolls these very green tea leaves
carefully into pearls,
hundreds of pearls an hour.

Snapshots of her unwind with the fragrance.
Her labor is inhaled
with the Jasmine scent.
I taste her anger and her love. Feel her longing.
I taste mine too.
We are awash in a hot sea of flowers.
A sea between, a sea of longing
we are awash in a sea of hot love.

White Spectacle

This mushroom swirls
out of the earth,
a single white spectacle
for a blind eye,
with news of the darkness
that surprises everyone.

It is a mystery we live
and relive
with every death,
the emergence of a white wing
arching from mulch.

Pin Point

Bobbin
of being is
weaving and
unraveling me
in one precious
and unpredictable
moment.

Sunrise Art Flight

This Eastbound flight
shows tiny silver threads
in the double-pane plexi.

Outside thin strips
of wooly air
are laid out for the weaver
and occasionally
block out the sun.

Lakes show up below
as shiny dimes on
gray-blue watercolor paper,
one continuous sheet of Fabriano.

Up here
the plexi-silver strands
have disappeared,
we see no birds
but our own shadow,
on the clouds, on the lakes

a flying shuttle
blending together the
random strands of wool.

Water Cradle

In the aft of the boat
I am tucked into the bunk
like a snail in a
Chinese soup spoon,

in a leaf floating.

My shoulders just fit
between broad teak planks,
legs follow the hull,
rocking with the tides,

through the open port hole
I hear the sea's gentle lapping
I hear ropes creek and halyards accent
the boat's gentle sway;

then dreams.

Seed Change

This body's a burning field
preparing me for planting
fertile seeds to flourish
seeds of praise.

My body is the charred earth
ash and loam swirl together
rain stirs them into food
stirs for beds of grace.

My body is drinking rain
soaking into steaming fields
to cool the naked fire,
cool trickling stream.

River of my cooling Earth
boiling to meet river rush
lapping each seed word free
seeds of poems.

The Sirens of Avila

They come with wet hot fingers,
loosening old armor
making the swimming easy.
You roll on your back
as they loosen your coiled shoulders,

locked in place by hours of driving.
Those Sirens lick every inch of silken skin.
You have traveled far enough,
too far for anyone,

They come for you again, back
into the heat over and over
until you are limp with their
voices, A-H-H-H-H.

Emersion

My bath is full of clouds
my breasts and belly
float to the surface
and rise like greasy
land masses.

Water full of salt
lemon and
oil of lavender,
soak out pain
from tired bones.

Painted toes poke
their odd heads out
of bubbles near the drain,
look like someone else's.

Precocious toes flip
the leaver that drains
all cares
and the scented water,
into the bay of
moonlit islands.

The Waters are Black Silk

My body is scattered,
floating.
I die
in a warm
silk-water embrace
over and over.

Hot black fingers seep in
to draw out the knots,
stored between bones
and flesh.

Bubbles of stars break
the heavy surface.
A sulfur ring,
the color of
sun bleached straw,
line the edges of this
long rectangular tub.

Laying aside
the past, I
sort it carefully
to stitch the wounds
so thick with pain.

It is time to heal
the days of
long ragged grasses
held in a fervor
not woven 'til now.

I Step into her Shadow

into the hot spring
where the old woman left.

Her memories remain
but not the sting,
I feel her umbra
but have no knowledge of her pain,

The heat and silk
of black water
invites me to disrobe too.

New Years Day Resolution

Morning sun
melts away frosted shadows
on the mountains.

Now, pelting rains
tap out windshield wiper beats
that match the turkey
vulture's lazy glide.

A wet red tail
fluffed and speckled
hunches on a fence post
and waits for the rain to stop.

Winding up the hill are
two paths. One worn
by foot and full of rocks
the other, a creek, flows with ease
and carves the earth
as it sparkles and gurgles
where ever the land gives way to it.

The rain stops.
I get out of the car
to walk up the
laughing path.

The Sound of Petals

Below golden bells
petals of tropical purple flowers
light up in shadows of Datura

They fall through broad leaves
and tangled branches

These petals carry a
clear and vibrant periwinkle light
bright in muddy shadows,
fading to magenta
as the sun dries them.

To me they are dark stars
glowing in shadow
triumphant particles
ringing, ringing
from those golden trumpets,

visible music
drips with hope
as stars fall through
night.

Cruising

Today a Blue Heron
floated before my car
her long neck tucked
into her neat "Z" fold.

Her wings held tight
to make double sails
for her drift then landing
on a nearby reservoir.

This elder at any age,
her graceful glide, head
high, landing smooth,
is my omen today.

This Emerald Man

You wear the healing leaves of Osaiem,
hobbles to me on one leg,
this wounded healer of the forest.
He embraces me with his spirit.

He is the one I have been waiting for.

Though my burns are tender
from decades of disregard, from Mother and
Father from lovers and finally from myself,
he gently holds me just the way I am.

He is the one I have been waiting for.

Because the neglect has burned me
gladly I receive the salve
of his presence
and the aloe he applies.

I know that he is the one I have been waiting for.

He hums a healing song deep into my bones,
gratitude rises as from a spring in the center of my being.
We listen, allow each note to carry us to the waters
of one heart deep in the forest.

Because we are the ones we have been waiting for.

The Promise of Attention
(or if I can do this, so can you)

After he left, after the
death of our daughter and the painful
years it took to recover, after hearing that
my dearest sister with cancer
has had more bad days,

I sit with all my feelings. The fear of loosing you
after she died, the outrage of being left,
I sit with the loss of more family, of your sons
that became my sons too.

So today instead of resisting more loss
I drop in.
On the beach I rest on a log, my
feet, legs, hips, spine
are wooden.
I do not push away or hold on
Just sit, in all the grief I've had,
the fear of more to come.

Then something wonderful happens
the fear of loss dissolves.

Deep in
the debris there is
a pearl, no, a
diamond
deep in my pelvis,
glowing.

It sits in an old wooden bowl,
for popcorn or bread, or cake
a bowl for mixing batter or bread
and opens into

a deep, deep calm
becomes the remnants of the hoped-for
diamond ring from a previous
engagement years ago,
which also dissolves
like my last marriage into
an inland lake,
expands

like the
vast
sky
or ocean

The light reverberates up my spine
into all the tight places.
All the paralysis
every tight fist in every muscle
that held on
lets go

But that is not all,
the diamond
grows, expands
into my whole being,
the tightness
opens up again and again

I relax into my body.
This temple
become the Taj Mahal
glowing at sunset,
before the sun turns alabaster
from silver to gold
the ocean gossamer blue

then fades and the
rays of the sun seem to vibrate
in every direction
until the salt and sea
and air and fire dissolve into

a constellation

a bowl of stars

empty-full-deep

clear

free!

On Fire
for Krishna

Flames sear away everything
but this love,

Sleeping or walking
you are here.

Dreaming of blue hands
eating watermelon,

Humming over and over
this word: one

A constant
waterfall.

My Hands Will Never Grow Tired

I will never grow tired
of these changes;
one walks a little faster,
another flies up the steps,
his face is pink again,
hers more peaceful,
another one blooms
with shades of roses
and someone else
fills up with hope,
yet
another finds peace
through acceptance,
and all we do
is just show up
and love them in the
dance.

Arrival

Born in a thunderstorm,
hail crashing,
lightning bolting all around,
my mother, the sea,
carried my little coracle
to the other side,
to the other side of her
broad thigh, to the other
side of the sea.

Family on both sides stood around,
stood around the shore
and I swam to Father's arms,
to Odin's arms
as he was hovering overhead,
hovering overhead.

And he said to me, My daughter,
my darling daughter, dear,
you shall be the one, the one, the one,
you shall be the one to carry on.
Your heart the sail, your body
the boat, your spirit will blow
your craft to inland shores,

My mother washed me, my father
wrapped me, and soon I was on
my way, how initiation flashes
and destiny dashes us, as we shape
our lives from foam, as
our lives are shaped from foam.

Before I started on my way
I could hear my father's echoing
as I stood on solid ground,

Be not afraid of anything
as you shall always know,
always know, always know,
you are being carried along,
carried along, carried along
You will be carried along
to where your destiny roams.

The Golden Bell

So this is what it's like
one moment fear
the next vastness.

Goals cease to be goals
instead a star-filled night
fills me.

Star Woman
you are me now
as you are every one.

No fear
now love
no contraction   now immensity

I am a dark night full of stars

Yet this is no night,
only shining,
no stars without immense space.

This spot called Earth
one elegant teacher of each
jasmine flower

Every scratch of
bird to its
flea bitten wing.

Stop, look how pink is sprayed through the rattan shade
as the copper sun lowers in the west
open to a single hum
a golden bell

calling one
to velvet
silence.

Self-Portrait as Star Woman

About The Author

Robin White Turtle Lysne

Born and raised in the Midwest, her work reflects the lanscapes of her first home in Rockford, Illinois, later in Michigan, and her love of California where she has resided since 1987.

    She has been writing poems for over thirty years, first as twins, coming out with her art work then on their own. The poems in this volume represent new and selected works over the last thirty years, though the span of time written about includes most of her life. She earned her M.F.A. in poetry from Mills College in 2012.

    She is the author of five previous books, the last one *Poems for the Lost Deer,* published in 2014, by Blue Bone Books, Santa Cruz, CA. Other books are *Heart Path Handbook, Heart Path*, published by Blue Bone Books, Santa Cruz, CA, and *Living a Sacred Life,* and *Dancing Up the Moon,* Conari Press, Berkeley, CA.

    In addition to her writing, Lysne is an artist who has shown widely from NYC to Santa Cruz, CA., with drawings, paintings, and handmade paper sculptures.

    As a professional medium, psychic and Energy Medicine Practitioner with 30 years experience she offers her clients safety, intuitive insight and compassion. In 2013 she earned her doctorate in Energy Medicine from The University of Natural Medicine, Santa Fe, NM. She offers trainings, and workshops on Energy Medicine and Shamanism giving others insight into the work of transformation.

    She is also the creator of Blue Bone Books which she started in 2006, which includes a collective poetry press.

    Today she lives and works in Santa Cruz, CA. and continues to write prose and poetry, sees clients, and teaches energy medicine. She has a novel and memoir in process.

Her websites are:
www.thecenterforthesoul.com and www.bluebonebooks.com

Acknowledgements

I have many people to thank for helping me shape these poems including; the late Margaret Albanese, David Whyte, the Emeralds Street Poets: Len Anderson, Virgil Banks, Phyllis Mayfield, Phil Wagner, Robin Straub, Marcia Adams, Stuart Presley, Lisa Simon, Maggie Paul, Janet Trenchard, Joanna Martin, Adela Narjarro, and Tom MCoy. In several workshops including Iowa Writing Conferences with Michael Carey, and Timothy Lui, Catamaran Writing Conference with Dorianne Laux, and independent workshops with Sally Ashton, I learned a great deal. From teachers in my M.F.A. program at Mills College, Stephen Ratcliffe, and Juliana Spahr, thank you for your support for *Poems for the Lost Deer.* Eternal gratitude for my cooperative press friends and fellow poets, Janet Trenchard, Marcia Adams, Stuart Presley, Lisa Simon, and Phil Wagner. Also Amita for her feedback, constant luminous support and insight.

www.ingramcontent.com/pod-product-compliance
Lightning Source LLC
Chambersburg PA
CBHW030437300426
44112CB00009B/1050